This Life I Live

This Life I Live

One Man's Extraordinary, Ordinary Life and
the Woman Who Changed It Forever

RORY FEEK

W PUBLISHING GROUP

AN IMPRINT OF THOMAS NELSON

© 2017 Rory Feek

Published in Nashville, Tennessee, by W Publishing Group, an imprint of Thomas Nelson.

Thomas Nelson titles may be purchased in bulk for educational, business, fund-raising, or sales promotional use. For information, please e-mail SpecialMarkets@ ThomasNelson.com.

Scripture quotations are taken from the New King James Version®. © 1982 by Thomas Nelson. Used by permission. All rights reserved.

"Nothing To Remember" words and music by Joey Martin and Rory Feek. © 2005 ole Black In The Saddle Songs, ole Giantslayer Music and Rufus Guild Music. All rights administered by ole. All rights reserved. Used by permission. *Reprinted by permission of Hal Leonard LLC.*

"When I'm Gone" written by: Sandra Emory Lawrence. ©2012 Ocotillo Red Music. All rights administered by Sony/ATV Music Publishing LLC, 424 Church Street, Suite 1200, Nashville, TN 37219. All rights reserved. Used by permission.

Library of Congress Control Number: 2016917201

ISBN 978-0-7180-9019-7

Printed in the United States of America

17 18 19 20 21 LSC 6 5 4 3 2 1

To Joey,
you forever changed my life
by letting me be part of yours.

CONTENTS

Contents

CONTENTS

One

FAMOUS FOR LOVE

I am famous.

Not for what most people think I'm famous for, though, which is music. Yes, I've written some songs that you've probably heard on the radio, and my wife and I have had a very successful career in the music business. And we've made half a dozen albums, toured the country and halfway around the world, and performed on television. We even had our own TV show for a couple of years. But that's not what I'm really famous for. Not anymore anyway.

I am famous for loving my wife.

—⁂—

There is hardly a grocery aisle that I walk down or a gas station that I pull into where I don't find a hand reached out to shake mine, an iPhone pointed my way, or, even more often, arms reaching out to hug me and to tell me how much they love me. And my wife. And my baby daughter and family.

Do you know what a gift that is? To know that millions of people not only have followed our story online through my blog and videos but also have sung along to our songs, and they've bowed their heads and prayed and shed their tears over my wife and me. Strangers have done this.

All of my life, I've been anonymous. A nobody. Now I'm not just somebody. I'm somebody's. I am Joey's husband, Rory.

And I am honored. So very honored to have been her husband. To be her husband still. To have stood beside her at the altar and be standing beside her still when 'til-death-do-us-part became something much more than a phrase in our wedding vows. To have put a wedding ring on her left hand. Twice. Once, in front of our friends and families that day in June 2002, and again in late February 2016, when we were all alone and the cancer had made her fingers so thin and frail that she had been wearing it on a chain around her neck, and she asked me to wrap masking tape around the bottom of that platinum promise so it wouldn't fall off her finger in the wooden casket that would be the final resting place for the ring with BOUND BY GOD FOREVER engraved inside the band.

But to know why being famous for loving my wife means so much to me, you have to know something more of my story. More of the journey than just the last two and a half years, which I have had the chance to share in my blog. More lyrics of the song that is my life. More of the darkness that I lived through to understand the light that I found and have had the chance to become.

My life is very ordinary. On the surface, it is not very special. If you looked at it, day to day, it wouldn't seem like much. But when you look at it in a bigger context—as part of a larger story—you start to see the magic that is on the pages of the book that is my life. And the more you look, the more you see. Or, at least, I do.

Two

STRONGER

I don't cry like I used to or hurt like I did when I was a younger man. I'm more stable. Stronger. Finally. When others don't or can't hold it together, somehow I do. I'm not sure why or when that started. I wasn't always like that. Far, far from it. I was an emotional mess most of my life. Crying and falling apart for the smallest of things. Most of them, things of my doing. Or things that were just in my head. I'm not like that anymore. At least not as far as I can tell.

—⚋—

We had a perfect at-home birth that, a few hours later, turned into a horrific surgery for my wife and a diagnosis of Down syndrome for our baby daughter. A few months later my siblings and I watched our mother pass away right before our eyes. And the year after that, I held my wife's hand as cancer took her, and I had to pick up our two-year-old daughter, Indiana, and somehow go on. But I have been strong. I have cried very few tears, especially in the moments where the pain lives or is learned. I have found myself crying in other moments. When I'm by myself— thinking, remembering, wondering. But all in all, I have mostly felt peace. My wife was the same way. She was strong in her faith and trusted God when difficulties would come our way. Just as I do. I don't know why. Or where I learned that. Or became that. I know that she is a lot of why I am me. Joey. And God. God that was in Joey. I could see Him in her. In her eyes and her smile, even when it hurt to smile. In her tears and her laughter, He was there. Her love strengthened my faith. And brought hope. Always, always hope.

It's a wonderful difference compared to how I used to be, but it's also unusual for me. Most of the people around me break down easily and often. Hope comes and goes like the wind. My sister Marcy almost didn't make it through my mother's passing. Her grief was so great. I couldn't relate to her. I tried to. I listened and was there for her and did my best to comfort her. But I didn't cry like she did or feel her pain. My view of our mom dying was compassionate but in a realistic way. People pass away. It's a part of life. It's hard and terrible, but it's gonna happen to all of us. Mom smoked, right up until the end, so this happens a lot when that happens. Somehow I could keep in perspective that Mom was seventy-one, and that's a long life. Still, even with that, I wonder if I should be crying or hurting more. I don't feel like I'm carrying a huge amount of weight or that I'm bottling up my emotions or anything like that. I just feel like I now have a different perspective from what I had most of my life. I have peace. Because of my faith. And finally opening my hands and turning my life over to God. Believing in a higher power and trusting that He has a bigger plan. One that I don't understand. That I can't understand this side of heaven.

God is the author of this story. Yes, it is my pen that He's used to write the book. My laptop, actually. But it's the story He has told with my life and my wife's. A story He is still telling. I just wake up every day and turn the page. Sometimes I'm frightened by what I find, and sometimes I'm exhilarated. Many nights I don't want to go to sleep and wake up the next day to turn another page. Afraid that the beautiful moment we're experiencing might be met with hardship in the next paragraph, and our journey to the top of a mountain will come barreling down the other side. But we must turn the page and trust that the story He is telling is bigger than that one page or that one chapter.

Looking back at my life, it is easy for me to see. Even the chapter that

I am in now, I know He is still writing. Taking my character and those around me, building a plot that is brilliantly woven into a beautiful tale that only the Master Storyteller could tell.

This is my story, up until now. Or at least a good chunk of it. Fifty-one years condensed into seventy thousand words. Mine is a sad story and a happy one. A human tragedy and a comedy of errors. It's Forrest Gump meets Jesus. The struggle of light against the power of darkness.

It is a story of faith. Of love. And a hope that never dies.

Three

THE MIDDLE OF NOWHERE

M y wife sees life like a garden. At least she did. I can't write about her in the past, so I won't. We will get to that, but for now . . . though she's no longer here, she's still here. In my heart.

—⁓—

Joey sees life like a garden. It's not something that she's said to me, or consciously would know that she does . . . but it's how she looks at life, how she sees the world and makes sense of it. Like all things, simply. Life is a cycle to her. A garden. God plants us somewhere. Then He gives us a spring filled with new life that is lush and green. Then a summer and an autumn and, ultimately, a winter . . . when the world seems to slow down and the life that was new in the spring comes to an end. I like that way of looking at this journey we're all on. It helps me to put things in perspective.

I was planted in the middle of nowhere—not because Atchison, Kansas, is nowhere or because it's roughly in the middle of the US, but because I'm not really from there. That's where I was born, where my first breath was taken, and where my spring began, but it's not where I'm from. I'm from nowhere and everywhere. Growing up, we moved dozens of times to different houses in the same town, and to different cities, big and small, in different states all around the country. Always putting down roots, only to have them ripped up at the surface with a part of me left behind in each place.

You try to replant, insert yourself in the new place, in the new soil, but you never really do. You can't grow, not really, when you know you'll be there only a short amount of time and have to move on. You hunker down for a bit, 'til you get your bearings . . . then peek your head up now and then to see what's around you, to see if it's safe to grow. But you always, always find yourself watching, waiting for that moment when you will again be uprooted and carried somewhere new in the backseat of a rusted Buick or Duster—to some new soil that may or may not accept you.

Part of me is in that river town in Kansas. That's true. But part of me is also just across the bridge in the dirty water of a lake in Missouri, beside an airport in Iowa, in a one-room schoolhouse in Nebraska, and various places in Texas, Michigan, and Kentucky. Broken pieces mostly. Scattered here and there. I get e-mails and Facebook requests from people who remember me from those places, who were there when I was there, from fans who say they "knew me when." I will be backstage at one of our concerts, and someone I don't recognize will tell me about the time when we did this or that. I politely smile and do my best not to let them see the lost look on my face.

I don't remember a lot about my childhood or early years as an adult. It's just not there. If our minds were computers with all information stored on hard drives, then my hard drive is corrupted, and no amount of "cleaning up my Mac" is able to retrieve those files. The details are there, I'm sure, somewhere . . . but I can't get to them. I just keep living each day and adding more memories that I most likely won't remember. Trying to add a special code to this one or that one, or highlight a file, but knowing it won't work. My mind does fairly well at being here but not being there. I wish I was better at remembering all the details of my past, but I'm not. I know people who are good at remembering, who can replay a single hour of a single day in fourth grade with perfect clarity. I wish I had been in fourth grade with them so they could tell me more about who I was then and what life was like.

So this book is not factual. Not completely anyway. It's a re-creation of some scenes in the story of my life, remembered and described to the best of my abilities. And like most things, when you add time and perspective, they become different. Better and more honest, I hope. You can sometimes make sense of something when you're on the other side of it. See something that you couldn't see before. You can see it for what it was, instead of what you thought it was while you were going through it.

This is my life as it was and as it is now—through the eyes of a man who has had some time to chew on it and live with the choices he's made for a couple of decades. I apologize if at times I offend or disappoint anyone. If I do, just know that I am disappointed in me too. But that's the point, I think. It's okay to have made mistakes. I have learned that all great stories must have a beginning. Where the characters are deeply flawed and in need of redemption and love. But as they move through life, they find that the things they once thought mattered suddenly become meaningless, and the things that weren't important become the good stuff.

My life today is filled with the good stuff. I know it is. Mostly because I've spent years trudging through the bad stuff and have learned the difference. The funny thing is that now, after all these years, even the bad stuff—in a strange way—was actually the good stuff. It's what got me to where I am. It made me who I am. And it will be a part of leading me to where I need to be.

Four

TRAILER TRASH

I like to say that I am from the good side of the trailer park.

People think that's a funny statement—the people who never lived in a trailer park do anyway. But if you had the good/bad fortune to spend a little time in a single- or double-wide, you know why that statement is true. No matter how far down the ladder of success you are, there is always someone a rung or two lower than you who's gonna help you feel better about yourself and your lot in life. My mom was proud that we weren't like "those hoodlum kids with no manners" who lived a few trailers away from us. Kids who didn't take baths and whose parents were in and out of prison. Never mind that Mom was sending us to the grocery store to buy candy with our government food stamps so she could buy a pack of cigarettes with the ninety cents in change we brought home. Or that she had us drive her car to the bootlegger's to buy beer for her, even though I was only fourteen and didn't have a driver's license, and our car didn't have tags, insurance, or brakes most of the time.

There are many different levels of poor. The best kind, I think, is the version I experienced. The kind where you're poor but you don't really realize it at the time. It never occurred to me that we had it bad and that other people, other kids in particular, had it much better than us. I don't know why, it just didn't. I don't ever remember being jealous of the kids on the school bus who were picked up in front of the nice houses in the towns where we lived, or of the clothes they wore or the cars their parents drove. Those feelings didn't come until much later. After high school, actually. I was just happy to be. I had a drawer with a pair of pants and three shirts in it and a pair of old cowboy boots. What else did I need?

We didn't always live in trailers, my brothers, Joe and Blaine, and sisters, Marcy and Candy, and I. We lived in houses too. And apartments. With aunts and uncles and friends. We didn't just move from town to town; we fled from state to state. Mom would do the best she could with what she had, but sometimes that wasn't enough. We'd find ourselves packing up and leaving in the middle of the night so our landlord couldn't catch us and demand the three months of back rent that was due.

When I was in the tenth grade, I came home from school one day to find that my Aunt Mary had come to visit. She and Uncle Rod had recently moved to Kentucky and were doing pretty well there. So when I arrived home that afternoon, I found Mom and Aunt Mary walking through the house with a stranger. They were looking at our furniture and the stuff in our bedrooms. When I asked my mom what was going on, she said, "We're moving." I asked her, "When?" And she said, "Tonight."

Late that evening we loaded everything we could fit into Mom's '74 Plymouth Duster and climbed in the backseat, with Aunt Mary navigating, as Mom, smiling as she smoked her Winston red, with the wing-window cracked, steered the car east for the latest new-and-better life that awaited in Kentucky. The rest of our belongings were sold to the auctioneer for three hundred dollars. And in time, it was a better life. It was always a better life.

The government apartment complex in Atchison, Kansas, was better than my uncle's basement, where we lived in Brownsville, Nebraska. And the green trailer in someone's backyard in Greenville, Kentucky, was better than the little house at Sugar Lake, Missouri, that we packed up and moved from that night in tenth grade. Though they weren't always better places to live, they were part of a better life to live. I don't think I knew that at the time, but I do now. It isn't about the house; it's about the home. And we were always trying to make one. Find one. My mom just wasn't good at it, I think. She didn't come from a good home, so it made it kinda tough for her to figure out how to provide one for her children.

Most of the time we didn't mind moving. We were used to it. We got to meet new kids and see new parts of the country. Sometimes it was a family reunion, like when we moved back in with Uncle Rod and Aunt Mary and their kids from time to time. We were just glad to see each other.

There's only one place that I wish we hadn't left: a small town in Kansas called Highland. We got there when I was in the fourth grade and stayed until the middle of my seventh-grade year. It was like something out of a movie, at least in my memory it was. All of us kids feel the same way. We loved that time and wish we could've stayed and grown up there.

My class had only seventeen kids in it. I don't remember a single name of the hundred kids I graduated with in high school in Kentucky. But I still remember everyone's name from my classroom in Highland. I remember those details vividly. What the streets looked like that I skateboarded down. How a Marathon candy bar tasted as you stood on the sideline, freezing at a junior high football game. And how Tina Scott played guitar in our music class that day. She was only nine or ten, but when she played and sang, I was mesmerized. I remember the smell of the gum in the football card collections sold at Ukena's Hardware Store and the feel of the tennis ball coming off my racket at the courts near Fifth Street. That court is gone now, as are most of the houses we lived in when we were there.

I've gone back to Highland many times. I still do. It somehow feels like home to me. I was there only about three years, but they were the best three years of my life. The truth is, I've spent my life trying to re-create one particular moment from when we were living there. We had rented an old farmhouse out in the country, which had a couple of old barns and a corncrib. Just down the lane was a creek where a bridge had collapsed, placing our house at the end of a dead-end road. I caught a million bullhead catfish and swam in a thousand swimming holes in that creek. Everything is bigger in those memories for me. Exaggerated. Probably because it was such a good time for our family. My mom and dad were back together, at least for a few months or so, and we were a family.

It was 1974, I think. Some of my memories of that time aren't completely clear. They're blurry and come and go, but they're very strong. Like the image of the number "38" on the top of a birthday cake that Dad was blowing out. Mom cooking fried chicken in the kitchen. Dad playing guitar on the couch, me sitting beside him, and him teaching me to keep time by tapping on the front of the guitar as he sang Jim Reeves's "Distant Drums." I remember a '55 or '56 Chevy in the driveway and forts being built in cornfields, a dog named Nooper that could climb the tree in the front of the house, and hours of going through the Sears & Roebuck catalog, carefully picking out Christmas gifts that would never come. Like the Pittsburgh Steelers pajamas I had at the top of my list . . . at that house, at that time, anything was possible.

I remember the smell of Ben-Gay and the feel of the football pads in the locker room underneath the stage at the end of the gym. And lacing up my first pair of Converse All Star tennis shoes. They were blue and white. The Highland Blue Streaks's colors. The color of my school. My town. I remember the sounds in the huddle as our quarterback John Paul Twombly called the play and told the receivers to get open. Then he looked at me, signaling that he was going to throw it to me, his best friend who played tight end. I was one of the best players on the basketball and football teams, and the prettiest girl liked me—or at least I thought maybe she did. I felt like I was somewhere that needed me.

But then we moved. First to town, then across town. Then finally far away. And I had to say good-bye to that place. To those people. I hated doing that. It's strange to say, but I never had a harder time saying good-bye than then . . . until this past year, when I had to say good-bye to my wife. That town meant that much to me.

I don't think my mom knew what it meant to me. To my brothers and sisters. Or she didn't care or, more likely, didn't feel that she could do anything to change it. By then Dad had left her again. Many more times, actually, in his usual creative way, with alibis and lipstick on his shirt or a brick through the front window of Mom's car. I remember hunkering down in the house on Fifth Street one night as Dad and Mom yelled and screamed, and he grabbed his half-empty whiskey bottle and slammed the door and left us. It wasn't enough for him to leave us; he had to maim us. Make it so that Mom was out of options. And pretty soon, she'd pull out some black trash bags and carefully fill them like fine suitcases with everything we owned. And we'd get picked up by an aunt or uncle and move on.

But part of us stayed behind. Especially in Highland. It was too late. Without realizing it, deep roots had grown into that soil, and though in the years to come, I might have been living in Avoca, Michigan, or stationed in El Toro, California, a part of me was still back there in that little town.

Why do you think I live in an old 1870s farmhouse now? Or drive a 1956 Chevy or play guitar and write songs and stories about small-town life? It's all part of getting back there. Finding my way back to that place in my head when everything was good, everything was right. And if it's true that we can't ever really go back, we find a way to bring the past into our future. At least that's what I did. It's what I think I'm still doing. Not on purpose. It just happened without me even noticing it. I woke up one day and realized that I have subconsciously spent my entire adult life trying to get back to that one moment in my childhood that I loved most.

Five

MAMA *BARE*

S he did the best she could.

That's it. All the years of being upset and disappointed by my mother and the choices she made came down to one truth: my mom did the best she could with what she had. And that truth has set me free.

For many years I struggled with understanding her, and I wanted some answers with regard to the tough times we experienced in our childhood. But the answers never came. Mom couldn't handle talking about the decisions she'd made in the past—about how they impacted us and how we still carry them around. I tried to get her to talk with me many times, but she would just shut down. She couldn't bear the thought that she had disappointed us or let us down. So for the last number of years, she acted as if it never happened, and that would drive me crazy. But, in time, I realized that it was probably a self-preservation thing. She knew. She knew her mistakes and failures far better than we did. And she had to wake up and carry them with her every day of her life. The weight was already heavy enough on her, I think. Having to face trial for it was too much.

So I learned to let it go—to just enjoy her for who she was and who she was trying to be. And that made all the difference in the final years. I loved my mom. I always loved her because she was my mother, but I loved her differently in the end. I was proud of her when the cancer finally took her from us. Really proud of her. I think it's hard to be proud of someone if you're angry with them. The bad emotions have a way of canceling out the good ones. So in the end, when I let the bad memories go, it made room for us to make beautiful new memories. That was hard for me to learn to do, but I did.

—⁕—

My mom, Rita Ruth Carnahan, was from a large Irish Catholic family in Michigan. Her father, Leo, was a hard man. He had been in the big war back in the early forties, and when he came home, he had a dozen children with his wife, Maddie. I never met my mother's mother. She died from brain cancer before I was born, but I'm told that she was a saint. By everyone. I've never heard a bad word spoken about her, which is a big deal—especially coming from a family who has a gift for talking about the worst in people.

My grandmother Maddie was a writer. I'm told she had poems published in local papers and that her writings still fill shoeboxes in closets somewhere at my great-aunts' houses. I once was given a story of hers that I still have. Typed beautifully. It's about a family trip Mom, her siblings, and parents took from Michigan to California in 1956. Stopping in Chicago, then Kansas, and continuing clear across Route 66 until they reached and saw the blue water of the ocean for the first time. It was beautifully written and filled with wonderful details. Clearly written by a mother with a passion to capture the moments that mattered in her life and to save them for eternity. I can relate to that.

My mom was difficult, I think. She had her own mind and wasn't afraid to use it. That was unacceptable to my grandfather. They butted heads early on and never stopped until he was gone. My guess is she had some unresolved questions for her father, just like I had for her.

By sixteen she was on her own, living with her newly married brother Rod and his wife, Mary—a routine that would repeat itself well into my teenage years. Mom had been married and divorced and remarried by the time I came along. Her first husband's name was Joe, and he was tough on her. Tougher than my dad was, I think. Joe beat her and left her stranded in California with a son in diapers who bore his name and another one on the way that he wouldn't meet until years later. Mom somehow found her way to Kansas and was waiting tables when she met my father, Robert. Tall and handsome, he played guitar and dreamed of singing at the Grand Ole Opry someday. He was a ladies' man. Unfortunately, not a one-lady man. That would cause problems in the future, but, for a while, it was good. Mom was pregnant when they met and fell in love, and soon after my brother Blaine was born, she found herself pregnant again. This time with me.

I was skinny with some red in my blond hair and a face full of freckles. My dad loved me. I know he did. He made it clear. He let me sit on his lap. That may not seem like a big deal, and it wasn't to me at the time. But it was to some of the other kids in the house. I didn't realize until years later that my two older brothers weren't allowed on his lap. My dad accepted them and provided for them, but he didn't treat them the same way he treated me or my two sisters who came later. He let them and everyone around know which children were his and which weren't. Which kids he loved most. How he didn't know that would scar those boys for life, I have no idea. But it seems he didn't. Or he didn't care. My two older brothers are in their fifties now, and both have had very difficult lives. I'm very proud of them and the men they've become in spite of their struggles. We look alike in some ways. Blondish hair, fair skin. But there's a hurt in their eyes that you won't find in mine. There's pain that is so deep in them, no amount of time or drugs or rehab ever touches it. Those things come and go, but the hurt remains.

Why my mom didn't set him straight, I don't know either. It was a different time, the late sixties and early seventies. Women were supposed to know their place, I guess, and so were stepkids. As a grown man, I can't bear to see people get hurt who don't deserve it—especially children. If I could go back to that time, when I was four or five years old, I'd climb off my dad's lap and push one of my brothers up there, and I wouldn't ask him if it was okay. I'd just stand there and dare him to say something. I'd like to think I'm that kind of man now, but as I child, I didn't even realize it was happening. I never saw it. I didn't want to, I guess. My father's rejection of my brothers didn't show itself like that. It showed itself through their failed marriages, prison sentences, and stints in halfway houses. And painkillers. Always painkillers. Even today, the doctors keep writing prescriptions for my two older brothers, but they can't touch their kind of pain. Medicine can't fix being rejected by a father. Only a time machine can unlock that door. Or an apology. And my father selfishly took that key with him to his grave. My mom tried to right the wrong over the years, but something tells me she needed an apology from her own father before she could see clearly to help her sons.

I'd like to tell you that things got easier for my mom, but they didn't. Trouble and hard times seemed to have found their way into our black-trash-bag luggage, and we carried them with us to all the new places we lived. She always struggled to make a living. To find love. To be happy. But there were good times too. She was proud of her children and believed that we were all destined for great things.

It wasn't unusual for me and Joey to be at Mom's house the day after we had received an accolade at an award show or event, and Mom would spend the whole time telling us how good my brother was doing, selling his homeless newspapers on the corner, or how my other brother was filing a lawsuit against his employers and would hopefully be getting a settlement soon. It's not that she wanted to hold me down. My mom just wanted to lift them up. She loved all her children the same, and she went out of her way to let me and everyone around her know. Funny, that was just the opposite of what my father did.

Most of my memories of growing up have to do with the tough times Mom went through, that we went through with her. Like the time when we were starving, living in a run-down government apartment complex in Kansas, and she had to break down and call my dad for help—asking him to pay just one month of the years of child support that he had managed never to pay. That call was hard for her to make. She didn't want to beg, but in this case it meant the difference between her kids going hungry or not. Next thing I knew, we were loaded in her car and headed to Kansas City to meet up with my dad.

When we pulled into the big, empty parking lot at the Kansas City International Airport that evening, Dad's car was already there. My brothers and sisters and I were excited to see him. Rolling down our windows and waving. Big smiles on our faces as Mom's car pulled in next to his. He just sat there in his long burgundy Buick, smoking a Winston. I don't think he even turned his head to look, pissed I'm sure that Mom had put him on the spot. He took another drag and kept staring into the distance, ignoring the excited voices and little arms dangling from our car window.

Finally Mom opened her door and walked around to the driver's side of his car. And then my father managed to take a woman who was at her lowest and drop-kick her to the curb. He rolled down his window a few inches, tossed a hundred or so dollars in small bills into the wind, and with that cigarette still hanging from his lips, slipped the Buick into drive and left my mother, with her babies watching, scrambling across the parking lot to pick up the cash. Anything that remained of her dignity was left there on that sunbaked pavement.

And it wasn't just my father. Most men in general were not good to my mother. When I was in high school and we were living in Kentucky, Mom had a job cleaning a rich oil guy's house. She cleaned his toilets, washed his dishes, and did his laundry while God-knows-what his wealthy wife was doing with her time. Sometimes in the evenings, Mom had to cook dinner and serve the couple and their uppity friends. She never enjoyed that, but again, if that is how she could make a paycheck, she did what she had to do.

But one evening in particular, I remember pulling in at their big fancy house to pick up Mom. She had been there late for another swanky dinner party they were throwing. Normally she came out tired and ready for her own beer and a cigarette. But on this night, she came out with tears streaming down her face. Sobbing. As we drove home, I asked her what was wrong, but she just sat there, staring out the passenger door window. She sat there for a long time, thinking. Finally she told me she had been fired. She said at the end of the party, she had gone to use the bathroom in the next room, and the rich man was listening from his seat at the table. He said he didn't hear the water running before my mom came back in the room, so he called her out in front of his friends. Said he couldn't have someone serve them who didn't have the manners to wash her hands after urinating. So he told her what a piece of crap she was and then fired her.

I'm sure that wasn't the first time Mom had been fired from a job, but even she knew there was no reason to belittle her in front of other people and make her feel so small. Sometimes I think it's the folks with higher education who are the most ignorant. I should've gone inside and stood up for her. Told that man to apologize to her. But I was still only about fifteen and my father's son. I had yet to come across any role models to show me what good men do. So I just drove, listened, and kept my eyes on the road.

Mom drowned her sorrows in Folgers coffee and Budweiser beer—every day, pretty much, for as long as I knew her—not together, of course. The coffee would take its shift from about six a.m. until six p.m. each day; then the beer would take over and get her through 'til sleep would come, and the process would start again. One would help her find courage to face another day, and the other would numb the nerves that were shot and the heart that was broken. Mom was probably what you'd call a functioning alcoholic. She would be disappointed to hear me say that, but I don't mean that in an AA sort of way. I mean it more in a descriptive sense. She just liked beer, and the alcohol seemed to help when nothing else would. I never once saw her stumbling drunk, but I saw a strange smile on her face some late evenings that you'd have a hard time finding during the day. It looked like happiness. Contentment. Or some form of it.

The story of men hurting Mom didn't stop with husbands, strangers, or boyfriends. Her sons were some of the worst offenders. Me included. One by one, each of us took our turns disappointing her with our choices in life. Sometimes they were in the form of bold-faced lies we told, married women we slept with, or calls that came in the middle of the night, saying, "I'm sorry, Mrs. Feek, but we've got your son in our jail." And sometimes they were worse things than that.

Mom just took it all in stride. Her kinda stride, that is. Chain-smoking cigarettes and downing twelve-ounce cups and cans. She had a stronger back than I did, that's for sure. With all the heartache that I've experienced, the weight on my shoulders has never been half the weight that was on hers.

On one scorching-hot afternoon in the summer of 2001, I remember sitting in Mom's trailer, whining about the tough day I was having. By that time, she was living just down the road from me in Tennessee, in an RV parked on a lot near the interstate. The RV didn't run, which was perfect because Mom wasn't going anywhere. She knew it too. Her life was at a dead end. Her three-pack, twelve-pack-a-day habits had stopped numbing her pain, and she was really feeling it. The emptiness had caught up to her, once and for all, I think. Unfortunately, I didn't notice. I had found some success, had written a couple of hit songs that played on the radio, and was complaining about something or other in the music industry and how this or that wasn't fair. Mom just sat there in that 150-square-foot trailer, smoking and listening. I was on a rant about my troubles when I looked up and saw a single tear rolling down her cheek. Like thirty years earlier, I asked, "What's wrong, Mom?"

This time she wasn't talking about the rich guy in the fancy house. She was talking about me. The rich guy in the fancy farmhouse. And sixty years of never standing up for herself rolled off her tongue. "I'd give anything. Anything. Just to live your life for one day."

She stopped me dead in my tracks. I knew what she meant. I wrote songs for a living. I was paid to be creative. My work was fun, and I was well compensated for it. She had just come off an all-night shift waiting tables at the truck stop on Exit 69. Her arthritis and age made it impossible for her to keep up with the younger girls and the boss who was riding her back.

Her tears started falling harder.

I got up and put my arms around her. And I held my mother—for the first time, I think. And tears fell from my eyes too. I held her, and she cried, and she let the truth of her life and mine run down her cheeks and onto that dirty gray indoor-outdoor carpet. "The only difference between me and you, Mom, is that I follow my dreams. I believe in something and move toward it, and somehow, it comes to be. Don't you ever want to be something, Mom?"

And she went on to tell me about her dreams. About how she had always wanted to go to college and be a writer. How she loved to learn and wished that she'd had the chance to do something, be something more when she was younger. But it was too late now. She was too old. Mom and I talked a long time; then I got in my new truck and drove away, thinking, *It's a shame that she never gets a break.*

But then she did. I mean, immediately.

I called Mom a few days later and asked her what was she doing, and like a dozen times in my childhood, she said, "Moving." I laughed and asked, "Where?" She told me that she was moving into a brick HUD house in town. That she had driven to the local community college and asked if there was any way in the world a sixty-year-old woman could enroll. It turned out that there was. She was a displaced homemaker who'd raised five kids. She barely made any money. So she qualified for a half-dozen grants and even government housing and a monthly check. The next time I saw Mom, we were moving her black trash bags into a pretty darn nice duplex in Columbia, Tennessee—the town closest to us. And at sixty years old, she drove herself to her first college class and sat with a hundred eighteen-year-old freshmen, amazed and excited at the new opportunity in front of her.

Two years later, all of us kids were there for her graduation. I've never seen a smile as big as hers the day she walked across that stage and they handed her that diploma for her associate's degree. Never. Except maybe mine that day and my brothers' and sisters'. We were all so proud of her, but I think she was the most proud. She, more than all of us, knew what it meant for her to get there. She had done something that no one—especially her—believed she could. I'd like to think that I played a small part in that change in her life. A part that I am embarrassed by, but a part in her beautiful story just the same.

Six

A HERO'S STORY

I think all fathers are their sons' first heroes. Some deserve it; some don't. My dad probably falls in the second category.

Dad didn't earn that title . . . with his bricks and whiskey and girlfriends and such. But still, I looked up to him. All of us kids did. And no matter how absent he was in our lives or how many times he disappointed us, he remained a hero in our eyes. I know that hurt my mother. She did all the work, and he got all the glory.

—⚭—

I'm what they call a romantic. I always have been. It's ingrained in me somewhere. Part of my DNA. It's the filter I see the world through, I think. My photographer buddy Bryan would say that my mind's camera has a lens that adds a vignette to everything—always casting a blur on the edges and taking the focus away from the parts of life that my mind doesn't want to see. That's pretty accurate. I'm like a modern-day Norman Rockwell painting, a painting of a painting that I'm painting. No matter how many layers deep you look into the frame, you see the same thing. It's not how the world actually is. It's a little bit better. A little bit kinder and a little bit sweeter. I choose to see the world that way. I think at some point I must've had to work to make a conscious choice to see life that way, but then after a while, I didn't have to work at it any longer. Now it just happens naturally, and I really can't see life any other way.

My father is part of that romantic vision. I have some black-and-white photos of him in the 1950s, standing beside Pontiacs and Oldsmobiles with large fins and girls with bouffant hairdos and names like Dolly and Beulah. His collar up and his black hair in a pompadour, like Brando or James Dean . . . only real. A member of our family. My dad. How could I not love a man like that?

There were times with him that were good: making the trip across the Missouri River Bridge for an ice cream cone or having breakfast at the Wagon Wheel Cafe. Playing baseball with him at Jackson Park and seeing him run to get on base. He ran like a man. Full of joy and wonder but still cool. Men were still men then. They didn't wear shorts and flip-flops like we do now. Dad was in jeans and nice leather shoes. Always. And a button-up shirt with his sleeves rolled up twice, revealing a tattoo on his forearm of a girl in a swimsuit, or a T-shirt that fit him well, even when his belly got a little rounder and the stubble on his jaw had some gray in it. He could be fun, and he had a great smile—something I still don't feel completely comfortable showing.

Looking at those old pictures, I see me in him. Him in me. Where my eyes meet the bridge of my nose. The same profile. The same brown eyes. And our passions are the same. Country music. Songs that tell stories. Old cars. And there are probably other things. Deeper things. My past lines up with his. He was a bit of a rounder, and I was too. Searching for love or acceptance or validation in someone else. I know that's still there. Still in me probably, but I've learned to desire and pursue more rewarding things. Things that Dad never seemed to do. Things like honor. Respect. Commitment to my wife and children. And God. That's the real biggie. I wish he could've known more of the good stuff before he passed away. Who knows? Maybe he did. And I just didn't get to see it. Or I can't remember it.

But I do remember him telling us kids that he was gonna take us to Worlds of Fun in Kansas City one weekend. He promised us. It was a local amusement park, much like Six Flags, and none of us had ever been. All of our friends had been numerous times and had told us all about it, and now it was our time. We were so excited. When the big day came, we were glued to the window; and when we saw his Caddy pull up, we dashed down the steps and across the apartment complex lawn and jumped in the car. He just sat there for a long time and didn't say anything. I'm sure we were bouncing around in the car, ready to go. Finally he reached over and pushed the button that opened up the glove box. He pointed inside. Then he proceeded to tell us that someone had broken into his car the night before and stolen the two hundred dollars that he had saved to take us. He said he was sorry, but there was nothing he could do. Then he just sat there.

We were disappointed, but we really didn't care about the amusement park. We mostly just wanted to be with him. But he didn't want to be with us. He just sat there and kept saying he was sorry, motioning for us to get out of the car. So we did. Soon all five of us were standing on the curb, watching him drive away, wondering what just happened. Trying to figure out why we couldn't have gone and done something that didn't cost any money, like going to the park or helping him do his laundry at a Laundromat.

That hurt me. It hurt all of us. And somewhere inside, that little freckle-faced kid vowed to not be like that with his children someday. Sad thing is, though, I was. I let my kids down. Many, many times. Maybe not the way Dad did, but in a hundred other ways. Times when I put my feelings and my needs and my emptiness first, above theirs. I went on making dinner or writing a song or dating some girl—leaving them standing on a curb, wondering why their dad really didn't love them.

The last time I spoke with my father, it wasn't good. It was November 1988, and I was in the service, about to be shipped off to Kaneohe Bay, Hawaii. I had thirty days' leave coming to me. Heidi was two years old, and Hopie had been born just a couple of weeks before. I called Dad from Memphis and told him I had some time and could come there to Kansas, and bring my wife and kids with me. He didn't say anything. In the background it sounded like he was watching *Jeopardy!* on TV, and maybe he was distracted by that. Or, more likely, maybe his own worries were overwhelming him. He had remarried, had lost a baby, and then had another son and an infant baby girl to care for. Dad didn't speak about his feelings to anyone that I know of—certainly not to me anyway. Chances are, he just had a lot on his mind. But he didn't share it with me. He didn't share anything. Just seemed uninterested. And so, for the umpteenth time, I hung up the telephone and said to myself, *I'm not ever calling or going to see that bastard again.* And that was that.

A few days later my little family and I were in our car, on our way east with no big plans other than *not* heading west to see my dad. By the time I stopped at some friends' house in Jacksonville, Florida, the phone was ringing. It was my mother, telling me that Dad had suffered a heart attack and died. I couldn't believe it. No one close to me had ever died. Yes, my father had died. But no one close to me.

A day or two later my sisters and I headed west after all. We went to his funeral, and we saw him there, lying in the casket. It was kinda surreal for me. I hadn't seen him in a year or two, and for the girls it had been even longer. I was twenty-three years old and had never been to a funeral, and I didn't know what took place at funerals or what was going on. I didn't know how to act. Was I supposed to cry? Or be strong? Was I supposed to touch his hand or kiss his cheek when the line I was in left me standing over his plastic-looking hands and face? I wasn't sure what to do. So I didn't do anything. I just observed. I can honestly say that I didn't cry over my dad dying. I don't know why. I guess it's hard to cry over the loss of something that you never really had. I've cried some tears over him in the nearly thirty years since then—mostly over what could've been, not what was. The truth of knowing he never got to see me realize his dream of playing the Opry and that my girls never got to know their grandfather and never will. That my wife Joey never got to meet him, and, even more, he never got to meet her and see what a lucky man his son was.

I remember the drive, in the long Cadillac, out to the cemetery on the hill where he's buried, and looking down at his grave and thinking, *I'm gonna make you proud someday.* And something inside of me reaching down and picking up the dream that he'd had for so long and carrying it back to Florida with me. Determined to make his dream—my dream—come true, one way or another. I remember that feeling.

But the truth is, his dream had already been passed on to me at an early age. I can remember riding in the passenger seat of his Electra 225, crossing over the railroad tracks in downtown Atchison, and him telling me about a new song that came on 61 Country on his AM radio. The song was "Farewell Party" by Gene Watson, and Dad wanted me to hear it, to hear the singer's voice, the words, and the steel guitar solo. And it wasn't enough for me to just listen. He pulled that Buick over to the side of the road, put it in park, and we sat there for the entire three minutes as the song played. He pulled over so I wouldn't be distracted and could hear every note, line, and nuance. Although I was only about eight years old at the time, I knew that song was a big deal to him. That music was a big deal to him. Important enough to sit on the shoulder of the road, listening with his little boy as the other cars and fathers and songs rolled on by. It was clear that country music meant a lot to him. So it soon meant a lot to me. Joey and I are friends with Gene Watson now and have played quite a few shows with him through the years. Dad would lose his mind if he knew that. I have no doubt he would be so proud if he were still here. But he's not.

They said he had high blood pressure. After he passed, his new wife, Linda, found some pills that I guess he'd been taking and didn't tell anyone about. But that morning in the fall of '88, the pressure and the stress of life was just too much. While standing at the counter, making a pot of coffee at four a.m.—his usual routine before he drove the sixty miles to work in Kansas City—he had fallen on the floor and died. He passed away right there in the kitchen, with Linda and their six-week-old baby asleep on the couch in the next room. She heard him fall and gasp for air, and she called 911. But by the time the ambulance came, Dad was already gone.

My sisters and I spent a few days in Kansas after his funeral. We rented a car and drove around Atchison, looking at some of the houses we'd lived in and the streets where we rode our bikes. Then we made the twenty-two-mile trip to our real home. Just on the other side of Highland, down an unmarked gravel road, stood the old farmhouse we all had loved so much. The roof was falling in, and the weeds were waist-high around the porches. But we had to see it. Had to go back and get one more glimpse of the place where the world was right and Dad was not only living but was living with us.

That house is long gone now. It's just cornfields. There's no sign that anyone ever even lived there. But we did. And probably quite a few families before us did too. I wonder if they made trips back with their families through the years like we did.

My kids know that old place well. I showed them the tree that the dog climbed and the room upstairs where my brothers and I slept with no heat. We even carried a wooden post and a broken end table back in the car with us one time. That end table sits beside my recliner in the living room of our farmhouse. And the post is holding up the drink stand at Marcy Jo's, the family restaurant down the street, named after my sister and my wife. Those things are part of the fabric of our lives now . . . reminders of a moment in time that we loved and how quickly it can all be gone.

My father loved me. I know he did. When I was in my late teens, I sometimes would make trips to see him when he stayed at the little truckers' motel in East Kansas City. It would be just him and me. And he loved me so much, I could feel it in his strong hug and hear it in the way he said the word *son*. He didn't have to say it. But he did. He liked saying it. He always told us he loved us. But saying it was easy. I wanted to *see* it. And that was something he wasn't good at.

But none of that makes him any less of a hero to me. Like my mother, he was doing the very best he could with the tools and the pain and the scars he had. I know that, and I'm not angry with him. I miss him and wish I knew him. Wish I *really* knew him. Thankfully, I can still see him from time to time. He shows up in the mirror while I'm shaving, in the way I talk with my hands, or in a dozen other parts of me. I am him. I am him, learning to be more. Hoping to be a hero to my children too. Hoping that when my time is done, I might have earned that role. Not by just telling them I love them but by showing it too.

Seven

THINGS THAT GO AWAY

My father's father's father's wife was full-blooded Cherokee. Or, at least, that's what I've been told. That would explain the black hair and dark eyes that my dad had. And his strong facial features. And, sadly, maybe his style of gift-giving too.

My father gave me a guitar one Christmas. Another time it was a gun. And once it was even a 1967 Ford LTD. He said he'd bought those things for me, that they were mine. But they weren't. They were still his.

Looking back now, I think, those things—like him—just stayed awhile, then went away. I don't know why, they just did. That 12-gauge was at my house; he'd given it to me. Said it was mine. Said that I was getting to be a man and that a man was old enough to have his own shotgun. I treasured it. From that one gift came a hundred dreams.

We lived in a small split-level house then, in a town near Omaha called Carter Lake, which was right next to the big airport. I spent my days studying the art of hunting. Dreaming of owning a bird dog so he and I could go on big hunts together. I read everything I could—every book, every magazine. I was going to have a yellow Labrador retriever that would pheasant and quail hunt with me. I would take my new shotgun and break state records for the most birds killed in one day and become known for training amazing bird dogs. I could see it. Of course, I was only thirteen or fourteen and couldn't drive yet, not legally anyway, so I just dreamed. We didn't live in the country, so I didn't know how I would get to the open fields or get a dog. I just imagined going there, being there, and that it would be great and I would be great.

Then one day I didn't have the 12-gauge anymore. Dad said he needed it back for something. I don't think he even told me why. He just needed it back, so it was gone. And overnight, my hopes and plans and dreams of birds and dogs and hunting also disappeared. I don't think I was upset. It was what it was.

It happened again with the guitar he gave me. I had always wanted to play guitar, actually felt like I was supposed to—not because of Dad but because of God or some intuition. He gave me that guitar one year for Christmas. Finding it under the tree was incredible. I tried and tried to learn to play it. What I didn't take into account was that you can't play a really cheap guitar. Seriously, you can't. The strings are too far off the neck, and it won't stay in tune—so no matter how much you practice or try, it won't sound good. You'll end up discouraged and disappointed. I did.

Dad asked for the guitar back a few months later. He said he had traded with someone for it, and the guy needed it back. I gave it to him, and it went away. And with it, my dreams of playing guitar. At least for a while.

The biggest gift, though, that Dad gave me and then took back was a car. Dad lived on Division Street then, in a tall white house with his new wife, Linda, and her young son, Josh. I was fifteen at the time and would visit Dad now and then, when he would come get us for a couple of days or when Mom would take us there and drop us off. One day when I got there, a beautiful light green Ford LTD that hadn't been there before was parked in the driveway. Dad took me outside, walked me all around it, and sat me inside. He told me the details of the car and said, "This is yours, son. I bought it for you."

My father would have an extra car in his driveway from time to time, and it was no big deal. As I remember it, he was buying and selling cars for extra money or something. Just one here or there. And usually only one at a time so he didn't have to get a car-dealer's license, I guess. So one day this Ford was there, but this one was different, he said; it was mine. He said he would keep it at his place until I turned sixteen, and then it would be all mine. I spent hours in the sun, washing it in the driveway, and many, many more evening hours sitting in the front seat or lying in the soft backseat, taking in that old car smell that Dad had taught me to love and listening to the radio until the battery would run down and the radio would turn off, along with the dash lights and everything else. I'd go inside the house, and Dad would be upset with me for running down the car battery, but it was all I had. I loved to sit behind the wheel and imagine myself driving down Kansas Avenue or pulling into the Dairy Queen and looking cool. Or driving across the country in my LTD and pulling into Nashville in the early morning light. Parking her at a diner, then going inside and sitting at a booth, like my father would, drinking my coffee, alone, admiring my automobile just outside the window in the parking lot. Imagining that the Grand Ole Opry was just down the street and I'd soon be playing there.

Then one day I came to Dad's house, and my car was gone. A different car was in the driveway with a For Sale sign on it. When I asked about the LTD, Dad said that he'd sold it. He didn't say it with any kind of emotion, just kinda matter-of-factly. He didn't say when or explain why he'd sold *my* car or apologize to me or even acknowledge that he'd sold the car that he'd given me. Honestly, I think he forgot he'd given it to me. Or, at least, he pretended like he did. And so, I guess, I did, too, and that dream and that car just went away. I think, maybe, looking back now, that those things were never really mine. They were still his. His gifts. The gift he received by giving them to me. And once that feeling wore off, he could just do something else with them. Again, I swore I'd never be like that. But, unfortunately, those patterns are hard to break.

In my late twenties I bought a mandolin for a girl I was dating and gave it to her for her birthday. She loved it and could play it pretty well too. I liked the feeling of giving it to her, and I could see in her eyes how much she loved the gift. And me. But months later our relationship became rocky and, ultimately, ended. When she broke up with me, I was crushed and hurt. So I drove over to her apartment and demanded that she give me the mandolin back. She did, but I could see that it hurt her. I didn't care. I was retaliating the only way I knew how. A gift isn't just a gift; it's a tool. I used it to try to win her love, and then I used it to try to hurt her, and it did. It probably still does.

I later gave that mandolin to my oldest daughter, Heidi, when she was still young, and all these years later, she still has it. I see it hanging on her wall or next to her bed when I come to her house to visit, and I'm reminded of what a jerk I was then. I could probably ask for it back from Heidi, and she'd probably give it to me, and I could return it to that girl and tell her I'm sorry and ask her to please take it back, but that wouldn't fix anything. The damage is done. All I can do is learn from it. And do my best to stop the crazy cycles that are inside of me.

I try to be a good gift giver now. I've been very blessed and feel a responsibility to try to be a blessing to others. To be generous when I can. It's my honor, actually. I can't imagine giving someone a gift these days and then taking it back. But that's not how I was raised.

Eight

UNCLE GOOMBAH

In the winter of my tenth-grade year, we were again living with my Uncle Rod and Aunt Mary. This time in a brick house on Highway 7, somewhere outside of Greenville, Kentucky. I had left my guitar and most of my belongings behind with the auctioneer in Missouri a few weeks before, so I was desperately wishing I had a guitar to play. Like all of my mother's brothers, Uncle Rod had a large Carnahan nose and a great smile. And he called everyone Goombah. I think it means "good friend" in German or Italian, or, at least, to him that's what it meant. In a closet in his bedroom, Uncle Rod had a beautiful Alvarez banjo that he played a little. He could do simple thumb-and-finger rolls and play songs like "Cripple Creek" and "Oh! Susanna," but that was about it. Though I had no idea how to play an instrument with only five strings, he generously let me spend my days trying to figure it out. I taught myself how to play three chords and was soon strumming it like a guitar and trying to write songs so I could sing along.

The banjo was a great substitute, but it wasn't the same as a guitar, and Uncle Rod knew it. But times were very tough, and Mom couldn't come up with rent for our own house, let alone buy a guitar for her youngest son to play. So I resigned myself to the fact that I might not ever have another one. But then one day my luck changed. Like most teenagers in the early eighties, my hair was long and feathered. Not sure how that fad got started, but it seemed that no one of high-school age was exempt from it. It started to get pretty unruly, so Aunt Mary took my cousin Aaron and me to get haircuts. Now, in Kentucky and most Southern states, there are lots of characters—and I'm a big fan of characters—people who are bigger than life, who take their own unique path and aren't ashamed of it. Bob Bethel, the fiddlin' barber, was one of those guys. He had a single-wide trailer where he cut hair, and while he was cutting, he was prone to breaking out his fiddle and playing a tune or two. I had never seen anything like it. I loved him right away. And lots of other folks did too. They would bring their instruments and hang around his barber shop and jam with him in the evenings or between customers.

The afternoon we were there, it was just him, Aaron, Aunt Mary, and me. And while I was in the chair with the barber cape on, I noticed a guitar case over in the corner, and I asked Bob about it. He brought the case over, opened it up, and showed me the Bentley guitar inside. I'd never heard of a Bentley before (probably for good reason), but she was a beauty. Dark brown stained plywood and imitation pearl inlays. He smiled and said, "She's for sale." I got a big grin on my face, but then he followed with, "Fifty bucks and she's yours."

He might as well have said fifty thousand. I sank back into the chair, and Bob finished my haircut. As we headed home, I rode in the backseat of that long Chrysler, deep in thought—having been so close to something I wanted so badly yet still so far away.

When we got home, I didn't say anything to anybody about it. Not even my mom. I knew she didn't have any money, and it would only hurt her to hear about something I wanted that she had no way to provide. So all through dinner and that evening, I was quiet—trying not to let the heartbreak show. Sometime after the dishes were done, Uncle Rod came in and asked me if I'd come back to his room. He said he wanted to show me something. So I followed him down the hallway to his and Aunt Mary's bedroom. When we reached the bed, he just pointed to a spot above the headboard and rubbed his chin. "The wall's missing something, don't you think?" he said. "A picture or a drawing maybe? The spot's too empty." I just nodded and told him I guessed so.

Then he snapped his fingers and said, "Hey, you've been doing some drawing, haven't you?" And I had. I was always drawing something on notebook paper or in a little blank pad that I had. Then he said, "Can you show me what you've got?"

We walked back into the living room and to the couch where I slept, and I pulled a few sketches out from underneath. He thumbed through them and when he got to one of an Indian beside a buffalo, he said, "This is it! It's perfect." Then he took off with it toward his bedroom. I wondered what was going on and followed him. He took a couple of tacks, pinned my drawing on the wall above his bed, and said, "How much would you take for it?"

I said, "Aw, it's free, Uncle Rod. You don't have to buy it." But he insisted. He pulled his leather wallet from his back pocket, fanned out two twenties and a ten, and handed them to me.

"Would this be enough?" he asked. "You'd be doing me a big favor. That empty spot's been driving me and your Aunt Mary crazy for months!"

Big tears filled my eyes. I said, "Really?"

He said, "Yes, son, really."

And just like that, I had a brand-new, cheap guitar to play. That guitar and that moment are a big part of how I've come to have the success in music and songwriting that I've had over the years. Because unlike many that I'd had before, that dream didn't have to go away.

I loved my Uncle Rod. He's my mom's brother. My cousin Aaron's dad. Aaron is now my manager and my best friend. His dad was the closest thing to a father that I had growing up. Like Bob Goff—one of my favorite writers—Uncle Rod had whimsy. He knew how to make life fun and could take the smallest event and turn it into something you'd remember for the rest of your life.

He did that again a couple of years later. He not only cosigned on my first car loan, but he also got me back on the road when I accidentally drove over a big rock that ripped the muffler system out from under it. But he didn't just loan or give me the money to fix it. He told me an elaborate story about how he'd been speeding on the way home from work when a cop saw him and hit the blue lights. Uncle Rod said he'd tried to outrun him through the back roads and cornfields and finally lost him as he pulled in the driveway . . . so, anyway, he didn't want to take his car to work the next day. He asked if he could borrow mine. I would be doing him a favor.

When he dropped the car back off to me that evening after work, it had a brand-new muffler and pipes, from the manifold to the bumper. And he didn't say a thing about it. He just did it, leaving another beautiful memory in the mind of a seventeen-year-old who desperately needed a man to leave one.

Uncle Rod died last year. He was seventy-eight. He went in for a routine heart-valve replacement and didn't come back out. My brothers, sisters, and I all either flew or drove to Oklahoma for his military burial. As a young man, Uncle Rod, I later learned, had been drafted into the army and spent a few years in the hell of Vietnam and brought some of that war back with him. In him. He was troubled but full of love. There isn't a room that my Uncle Rod walked into from here to California that he didn't light up with his smile and his laugh but mostly with his love. He touched a lot of lives, including mine.

On a gravel road outside a power plant in Paradise, Kentucky, he gave his son Aaron the big "sex talk," knowing full well that I was sitting on the other side of his son in the front seat. And when Aaron and I found ourselves in the Muhlenberg County jailhouse, it was Uncle Rod who came in the middle of the night, bailed us out, and told us that he expected, no, that he *hoped* for more than that from us. And on the day I left for Marine boot camp and gave hugs to my mom and Aaron and my brothers and sisters, it was Uncle Rod who pressed into my hand a piece of paper with a typewritten note to me that I still have to this day. He knew that there are times a boy needs a father, and when that father isn't around, it falls on the shoulders of the next man in line. Again and again, Uncle Rod proudly took the role of surrogate father in my life.

Rory,

Take pride in your background,

Take pride in yourself,

Take pride in your Country,

Never take the freedom you
enjoy for granted.

Choose your friends wisely,

Then be there when you're needed.

In your work and in your relation-

ships, take care of the little

things and the big things will

take care of themselves.

And most of all, remember that

your family love is unending.

Enjoy and Grow

Love, *Uncle Rod*

Before my time down here is over, I hope to make that kind of impact on someone. To have the gumption to not just help them but to go to elaborate lengths to make them part of a bigger, better story, like Uncle Rod did with me.

A story that will live long after the man who told it is gone.

Nine

FROOT *LOOTS*

D id I mention that I robbed a train one time? It's true. No, it wasn't at gunpoint, though a gun was involved.

I do my best to play up that line when I can. Being a country music singer, aspiring to follow in the footsteps of Johnny Cash, Merle Haggard, and others, I'm somewhat proud of the fact that I can tell folks that I once robbed a train. I usually prefer not to go into any of the details of the event, not because I'm ashamed of them (although I should be) but mostly because the details sorta change the power of my "time spent in the big house" testimony.

I was about fifteen years old, tall and gangly, still newly living in a little green trailer in the backyard of a nice older couple who lived right near the edge of Greenville, Kentucky. My cousin Aaron and I didn't know many people yet since we'd both recently moved there and were pretty shy. Luckily, on the bus to school we made a new friend who was a fast-talker and much cooler than us. His name was Scotty, and as it turned out, he was a preacher's son. That should be safe enough, I'm sure my mom figured, but not hardly. It seems that the children of the men who lead churches tend to like to lead lives that are a little different from the ones their parents preach about. This one did, anyway.

In the first couple of weeks, we started hanging around with him, we learned how to break into empty buildings at night using an unlocked window instead of a key; how to climb onto the roofs of other buildings, rip off the shingles, and throw them at passing cars; and even how to get free candy from vending machines by knocking them over. Once the glass shattered, we just tipped it back up, and everything was free. I am not proud of those things. But they happened. Those things and the Great Train Robbery of 1980.

Aaron, Scotty, and I had a hideout. Well, it was more like a ditch where we hid some beer that another friend named Bruce had stolen from his old man. It was pretty lame . . . a spot in a field where we would sit and talk; no one was around, so, technically, I guess we could call it our hideout. On one particular day we were walking down an alley and came across some grain bins near a railroad track. We proceeded to climb up on top of one and let ourselves in through the metal hinged door, then just sat in the big pile of corn that was inside. I played my harmonica until I accidentally set it down and lost it in all the corn. We eventually got bored and climbed out, looking for something else to do. Scotty recommended we open the doors of the train boxcars parked nearby and see what was inside. We thought, *Sure, what the heck?* So we took a pocketknife and cut through the little tab that said something about "private property" and "federal offense" and slowly opened the first boxcar door.

The first car was filled to the brim with cardboard boxes. We opened up one. Ketchup. Sixty million cases of Del Monte ketchup. We quickly tried another. Green beans. We bailed on that one too. Then we hit the mother lode. A boxcar filled from floor to ceiling with cases of Froot Loops. We dug in and stayed awhile. We laughed and talked and ate 'til we were almost sick. Then we decided we'd take a case each and maybe stash them at our hideout ditch, just down the alley.

Unfortunately, about a hundred yards into our trip, we heard a car come barreling up behind us, blue lights flashing, so we dropped our loot and took off running. Halfway down the alley I peeled off to the right and ran around some houses, then found a spot between some bushes and somebody's front porch. I wasn't sure where Aaron or Scotty were until I felt Aaron land on my back. He and I just lay there in the dirt, listening to the sounds of our heavy breathing and the police radios saying,

"I think they went this way!" and "Any sign of 'em?" Then we heard a gunshot. I checked to see if I was still breathing. Or dead. The adrenaline was pumping through my veins; I was so scared. Then suddenly the barrel of a pistol was against my cheek, and a knee was in my back and Aaron's. I heard a voice say, "We got 'em. Over here!" And the next thing we knew, we had handcuffs on and were in the backseat of a squad car.

Now, I hadn't ever been to jail or seen police officers up close, but I'd seen them on TV, and I'd seen what happened to suspects, and I could see my future. Seriously. I could almost feel an immediate shift in what was going to be the story of my life. I was going to be a hoodlum, and spending time in jail was gonna be normal for me. I hung my head and sulked as they drove us downtown, and so did Aaron. At the jailhouse it was much the same. He and I thinking we'd become hardened criminals for a few boxes of Kellogg's cereal.

Maybe fifteen minutes or maybe three hours later, I don't know, an officer came and got us and told us he was taking us to the police chief's office and that Aaron's dad was on his way too. We each took a chair in the corner of the room and slunk our bodies way down low in the cushions, upset at how we'd been treated. Those officers had used curse words at us. Bad ones. And told us we were lying when we said we had never done anything like this before. I thought to myself, *Wait 'til Uncle Rod gets here. He's gonna set them straight! They'll be sorry for arresting and being so tough with us.*

But when he got there, it didn't go the way I thought it would. Uncle Rod just listened as the gray-haired man with the stripes on his sleeves told him what we had done and that someone had been breaking into the boxcars over the last few months and stealing things. More than just cereal. And he told him that this was a federal offense. We had broken a railroad seal and could go to federal prison for our crime.

When the chief was finished talking, I expected Uncle Rod to lay into him. To tell him he couldn't treat his boys like that, and that we were innocent until proven guilty. I even thought maybe he was gonna sue the city for the hardship that they caused us. But he didn't. Instead, he just said, "Excuse me for just a moment." Then he turned to Aaron and me and said, "Sit up. You boys show some respect to this man and the difficult job that he has to do." Aaron and I bolted to attention in our chairs. Then he asked the police chief if he could take us for a drive, to talk to us. He said he'd be back in an hour. By then it was two in the morning, and, surprisingly, the chief said, "Okay. Have them back here in an hour."

Uncle Rod drove us back to the scene of the crime and while driving said, "They want you to tell them who the other boy was that was with you. They'll let you go if you tell them who you were with." Both Aaron and I were hardened criminals by now, and Scotty was our friend. We would never rat on a friend. But then Uncle Rod said something that would devastate even the hardest criminal: "I'm disappointed in you boys." And we caved.

Through the tears pouring down our cheeks, we told him it was our new friend Scott, and since he said he had done it before, we didn't think we would get into any trouble. We were so sorry. Then he asked, "Where does he live?" And the next thing we knew, it was three in the morning, and we were knocking on the door of the preacher's house next to the big Baptist church. An older, balding man and his wife came to the door in their nightclothes. "Tell them," Uncle Rod said.

So we told them the story and about how we'd been in jail most of the night and how the other boy had run off in a different direction. We were sorry, but we had to tell them the truth—the other boy was their son. They were horrified. They didn't believe us. They called up the stairs to Scotty, and he came down, wiping his eyes as he stepped to the door and saw us. "Hi, guys," he said. "What's going on?"

Scotty denied the whole thing. He said we were bad kids from another state and were making it all up. I don't remember what happened after that. I think we got community service and Scotty got away with it. But one thing I do know: we weren't friends anymore. Just like that, we were out of the club.

I saw Scotty years later on a trip to Kentucky. It was around a bonfire. He was in his thirties, handsome with a big smile. He was a car salesman or a preacher or both. I can't remember. But he seemed like a really nice guy. We sat around the fire that night and laughed about that story together. I think God had been working on his character, like He had been working on mine.

We all get the chance to be someone else. To start over and put the past behind us. And God gives us another one every day. I love that.

A few years later, when I was seventeen and joining the Marines, they almost didn't let me in because I had a felony charge on my record somewhere. Then they almost didn't let me in when I explained to them it was for robbing a train . . . for Froot Loops.

Ten

NASHVILLE

M y first trip to Music City was a disaster. I darn near starved to
death and quit playing music forever. All in thirty-six hours.

—◊◊—

I love this town. Nashville.

I have spent the last twenty years chasing and grabbing hold of my
dreams and seeing most of them come true in bigger and better ways
than I ever could've imagined as a youngster. Nashville has been my
home for two decades. Whether living in an apartment complex in the
suburbs of Bellevue or in the big white farmhouse forty-two miles south
of the streets of Music Row . . . Nashville is home.

My first trip to Nashville was not a great one. Though I had dreams
of arriving there, guitar case in hand, taking the town overnight and the
music industry by storm, it would be years before I would get the chance
to try and fail.

It was the fall of 1982, and my sister Marcy and her husband-to-be,
Phillip, made the hour-and-a-half drive from where we lived to drop me
off at the Nashville airport. I was to fly to Texas to visit my brothers. My
oldest, Joe, was having big success, or having some trouble—we weren't
sure which yet. He evidently had come into some money in his new

business and wanted me to come visit. Blaine, my next oldest, wanted me to come help him figure out what was really happening.

On a collect call days before, Joe had said he was going to wire a plane ticket for me to fly to Dallas, and it would be waiting for me at the airport. All I had to do was get there. He would take care of everything else once I got off the plane in Texas. So I waved good-bye to Marcy at the Nashville airport, and they pulled away, and I was off on a big adventure. I had no idea how many things could go wrong, and in the era before cell phones were invented, and with no phone at our family's house, it would get even harder to figure out what to do.

I made my way, with a yard-sale suitcase and a guitar case carrying my prized Bentley guitar, to the American Airlines terminal and found a spot in line. When I got to the counter, I told the lady that my brother had bought a ticket for me. I gave her my name, and she searched her records but didn't find anything. I asked her to try again. The flight wasn't for another hour and a half, so she told me to come back in a little while; maybe it just hadn't come through yet. So I found a seat nearby and waited. When I tried again, there was still no ticket. Soon that flight left, and I was still there. I got in line for the next flight that was headed to Dallas, and the same thing happened. Then I tried a different airline but still nothing. So I just waited. I had six dollars and some change in my pocket, and two phone numbers. One for Joe and the other for a house where Blaine was staying with his girlfriend.

Every hour or so, I picked up the pay phone and tried making a collect call to the numbers. No answer. Again and again. The next day I was still there, and starting to get worried. I spent two of the dollars on candy bars and Mountain Dews and was starting to get really hungry. I had no way to pay for a meal and no way to get ahold of anyone back home or where I was going. Finally, at the end of the second day, my brother Joe answered. He said there must've been some mistake because he had paid for the ticket. Then he said I needed to head to the bus station. He would have a ticket waiting for me there. I asked how to get to the bus station . . . I didn't know where it was, and I had a feeling it was a long way away. He told me to catch a cab and that he would put some extra money in with the ticket that I could use to pay for the taxi.

So that's what I did. I waved down my first taxi and rode the ten miles or so to the Greyhound bus station in downtown Nashville. The driver was a middle-aged black man who asked me if it was my first time in Music City. I told him it was and shared with him how there had been a problem with tickets and how my brother was getting me a bus ticket instead. He watched me in the rearview mirror and listened. Skeptically, I'm sure. Probably knowing better than I did that he was about to get stiffed. When he pulled into the busy downtown station, I told him I would run in and get my ticket and come back out and pay for the taxi ride.

When I got inside, there was a long line. I had been carrying my suitcase and guitar for two days and needed a break. So I sat them down beside a bench and got in line. It took a few minutes to get to the counter, but just as the lady said, "Can I help you?" out of the corner of my eye, I saw a man pick up my guitar case and take off running. He bolted through the front door before I could even figure out what was going on, and when I turned back to the lady, she said, "You need to keep your things with you at all times, sir." I went and grabbed my bag and came back over. She could tell that I was heartbroken. "You're not from around here, are you?" she asked.

"No, ma'am, I'm not," I said. And I told her about the airport and the mix-up and how my brother had sent the ticket here and how there should be some extra money for cab fare and for food. She looked up my name and said, "I'm afraid someone is pulling your leg."

Beyond brokenhearted, I made my way over to the bench again to find a place to sit down and die. Then, looking out through the front door, I saw the cab driver. And I remembered. *Oh God, what am I going to tell him?* But when I saw him come in, he was carrying something. My guitar case. He had seen the man run out the door with my guitar, and he chased him down the street and got it back for me.

I didn't know what to say. The cab driver made it easy for me. "It's okay, kid," he said. Then he wrote down his name and address and said if I ever got any money, I could send him the cab fare, and he walked out. I so wish I still had that piece of paper. I'd like to go back in time and send him a thousand-dollar bill. Instead, I lost that paper, along with all hope.

I tried my brothers a few more times from the pay phone there. Joe never answered. But Blaine did. He explained that this was why he needed me to come to Texas. "Something's going on with Joe, and it's not good," he said. Blaine and his girlfriend found fifty dollars and had a bus ticket wired to me, along with an extra five to buy something to eat. By the time I got to Texas, I had probably dropped ten pounds from my already-rail-thin 140-pound frame. I can still taste those eggs and that bacon I had when I arrived in Arlington. Wolfing it down and asking for more. Man can't live on candy alone . . . but I gave it a good try. All I'd had to eat was Snickers bars and soda for almost five days.

It was good to see my brother Blaine. And even good to see Joe when he finally came around, in his hundred-dollar track suit and driving a brand-new Camaro.

I soon learned it was hard drugs that Joe had come into, not money. And that caused him to believe he had money when he really didn't. I was still only seventeen at the time and didn't understand much of the world. During the two weeks I was in Texas, I became more confused than ever. But for now it was enough just to be somewhere I was needed, even if it was to help get my older brother arrested so he could get some help.

The next time I would come to Nashville, I would again have a guitar in my hand, but I would be older. Wiser. And though I would find crooked sharks ready to steal my music and people who'd promise me money and never come through, I would be more prepared. I was going to take my time getting there, so once I got my foot in the door, I'd never have to leave.

Nashville would be my town.

Eleven

JOINING UP TO SING

—⚍—

H is name was Gunnery Sergeant Bell, and God placed him and me in exactly the right, or wrong, place at the right time.

—⚍—

At seventeen, after graduating high school a year early, I worked a few odd jobs around the little town in Kentucky where we lived: painting handrails and hallways at the junior high and mowing the schoolyard. But soon I found myself bored and ready to begin life. Ready to find my way to Nashville, even if it meant taking a few detours on the way.

My brother Blaine had joined the army the year before and was back home now in the Army Reserves, painting houses and going to meetings one weekend a month. He told me lots of stories about boot camp, how they had weekends off, how the drill sergeants were hard, and how it had changed his life, and I could see that it had. I could hear it in his voice with every story he'd tell.

So I decided I'd join the army too. My dad had been in the army back in '59 and '60, and though he said he was trained as an artilleryman, he had been given the chance to play music for his job and even played guitar for Steve Lawrence one time. His stories were so romantic, and I had seen a few black-and-white photos of him in his uniform, doing push-ups with his buddies and with pretty girls on his arm. I decided that was the life for me. I would serve two years, like Dad, save a little money, then get out and move to Nashville to pursue the fame and fortune that surely awaited me. All I had to do was take a few tests and sign on the dotted line. I took the tests they give all prospective recruits and did well. The Army Recruiter told me to come back on Saturday, and we'd be all set. I could ship out for my basic training.

The following Saturday afternoon, I made the twenty-two-mile drive to Madisonville and walked into the recruiting office, but the Army Recruiter's door was locked. No one was there. I was disappointed. Before I could even register what to do next, I heard a voice behind me say, "Have you ever thought of being one of the few and the proud, son?"

I turned to see a huge hulk-of-a-man in a dress uniform with an eagle, globe, and anchor on his collar. "I'm going into the army," I said, and I turned to leave. But he stopped me and asked if I'd sit down and talk to him for five minutes. *No problem*, I thought. I had done enough research to know that the Marines didn't have two-year enlistments, and besides, they were the toughest branch. I wanted a walk down easy street, same as my brother, but I figured it wouldn't hurt to listen. *I'm gonna do two quick years in the army. He ain't gonna change my mind.* Little did I know, he would.

He started the whole conversation by saying, "What do you really want to do, kid . . . more than anything?"

That was the wrong question, I thought. *Once I tell him, he'll realize he's talking to the wrong guy, and I'll be out the door and headed for home.* "I want to play and sing country music," I told him, as I reached for my coat . . . sure that our conversation was over.

But he stood up before I could leave and said, "Wait here." He walked out of his office, then into the parking lot to his car. Then he popped open the trunk and pulled something out . . . a guitar case!

When he got back inside, he opened the case and started strumming. He and I sang Merle Haggard songs all afternoon. By five p.m., I was signed up for the Marine Corps for four years of active duty. All because he played guitar and loved country music as much as I did.

I had no idea how ridiculous that was, and I wouldn't really come to my senses about it until I was in boot camp a few months later as the drill instructors threw trash cans down the center of the barracks at four a.m. each morning to wake us up. I started to wonder if maybe I should have looked into this a little more before signing on the dotted line, right after a chorus of "Silver Wings."

The truth is, I love that story. I love that that's how I enlisted. It was foolish and silly and perfect. And it was also naive and innocent, something that wouldn't be a part of my life for too much longer.

Twelve

YOUR FIRST TIME LASTS

I was eighteen, and it was my first time. I don't think she knew that. Maybe she did.

It wasn't special. It wasn't good. Honestly, it wasn't anything. It was in a car parked beside a long-closed gas station. She had ten minutes, she said, before she had to be back home. I wouldn't need a tenth of that.

She smelled of cigarettes. I hated that smell. I had grown up with it everywhere. I should've known it would be there for that too. I had met her a couple of years before; her family played music, and I'd been around them some in high school. She was older than me, and I think she had a boyfriend. A few of them. Some guys picked her up on Harleys, and they went away for weekends. She said they were just friends, and I believed it at the time. I didn't know any better. I thought that, maybe, what she and I had was love.

But it was clear in the front seat of that car, that wasn't love. It was something, for sure. But not love. I didn't see her much after that. Not sure why. Maybe that experience with me disappointed her, or me. Either way, it didn't matter. It left me more confused than ever. I had a wound. I wanted someone to love me. I wanted to feel love, be loved by anyone. Anyone who would have me.

It isn't that my mom didn't do something or give me something that a young boy needs, and it wasn't some deep-seated thing from my past that caused it. It was just always there. Like it was in my mom. And my dad, probably, and my siblings. The need to feel needed. At any cost.

I could've fallen in love with lots of girls in high school, but I was shy. Really shy. And I didn't know how to get from here to there. From sitting beside a girl in art class to holding her hand at a basketball game. That was a valley I could never seem to cross. Actually, I fell in love lots of times, but the girls didn't know it. One did. Kim something-or-other. We went steady for a little while during my junior year, and I really liked her. But I came home one day from visiting my dad at his house in Kansas, and my brother Joe was sitting on the couch, holding Kim's hand. And that was that. I don't think I ever knew what happened. They were just together, and we weren't.

—⁂—

After I joined the Marines, I started to learn more. A lot more. The guys would take me out drinking, and we'd end up at a drive-in theater, watching some movie with lots of skin and no plot. It was pretty eye-opening for me. I'd been fairly sheltered overall, I think, compared to most of them.

We had some things happen when I was young. Things that weren't good. I had. All of us kids had. Experiences with neighbors or strangers that shouldn't happen to kids. But those were hard times, and there was really no one around to watch us and keep us from such things. Mom was busy trying to make a living and find her own self-worth, so we had to figure out a lot on our own. I don't blame anyone, and I don't let any of those things affect me or use them as an excuse for who I am or who I'm not. But I know they left scars. Inside. Deep down. Wounds that you can't see with your eyes. Gaping holes in my soul that I've spent a lifetime trying to fill with sex and booze and fame. You can have all those things and still be empty. I know. I've been there.

My second time was better than the first. And a hundred thousand times worse.

She was married. To a friend of mine. I was home on a weekend pass from the service, and some buddies and I stopped by to visit them. My friend wasn't there, but his wife and their two kids were. Little boys, around two and four. She asked us to stay awhile and visit. Her husband was on a job a few hours away and was gone for weeks at a time. She was bored and lonely and would love some company. We thought it was a good idea. But it wasn't.

Everyone was drunk. Me included. And then it happened. By the next morning, she and I were sitting at their kitchen table, and she was asking about the future—what we were gonna do. *We.* She said "we." No girl had ever included me before. I said I didn't know. She told me that we should come clean, that we were in love and should let everybody know it. I was still drunk. Exhausted. Reeling from what had happened the night before. It had felt like love, compared to the time with the girl and the smoke in the car. Maybe it was. I looked up and saw my friend's wife looking at me like she cared about me. I said, "Okay, let's do it."

Over the next six months or so, I proceeded to break my family's hearts and hers into a thousand little pieces. And that man. My friend. He cried a million tears for his wife and his babies, who left him to be with me.

In the end it didn't work out. She woke up one day a thousand miles away in an apartment with me and realized that she didn't love me. She still loved him. My friend. Who was now a long, long way from being my friend. And so, with tears streaming down my face, I took her and those little boys to the airport and watched as they boarded a plane to try to go back and resume the life they had. Meanwhile, mine had been wrecked.

I wouldn't get over that for a long time. They were gone, but the truth of it stayed in me. Not only what happened but also who I was—that I was the kind of person who would do that to someone else. I hated myself for it.

Thirteen

FORGIVEN GREATLY

I've spent my whole adult life hiding this story. Being embarrassed and ashamed of it. Now I'd be ashamed not to tell it.

I have to tell it if I want the chance to tell you how it ended. To tell you about being forgiven and why it has become easy for me to not hold grudges, to let things go, and forgive others. That's actually what the story is about. The part where I did everything so wrong, as it turned out, was just the beginning of a bigger story. Just the setup. For years I thought that was where it ended—the part where I was at the airport in tears, facing the truth that I had ruined my life and some other people's. But it wasn't.

There was going to be more. Or, at least, there could be. A different ending. There always can be a different ending to the story you've been telling. You just have to follow that still, small voice inside of you. And do something to change it in order to write about it.

I also have to tell you about this story so you can understand how incredible it is that I am famous. Not just famous. But famous for loving my wife. It's an incredible thing to be known for that, but it's even more incredible knowing where I came from, knowing what I could've been known for. That is the power of change. Of God. Of the amazing truth that in the blink of an eye, He can take a world-class loser and turn him into a world-renowned lover of someone, if you put your trust in Him and follow where He is leading. I am humbled by this story, by how it

63

ends . . . actually, how it is still unfolding. That is why I remain in awe of Him and what He has done in my life and why I try hard to be an open book in sharing our story. Because I know what He's done in my life, and what He delivered me from.

—⁓—

It was 1994 or 1995, I think. About twelve or thirteen years after that scene at the airport. I was back home, visiting family. My kids were maybe eight and ten years old, and I woke up one morning thinking about my friend, about that time, about what I had done. I hadn't thought of that incident in years. I had moved on, and life had turned out pretty good, overall, but still I carried it with me, down deep, and it was always there. On this particular morning, the memory of that time, those mistakes I made . . . wasn't just down deep, it was upon me. Everywhere. I could feel it calling from inside of me. It wanted out.

Something in me was aching for resolution. But how? Some things can't be fixed. No amount of time or prayer could undo what I'd done. I knew that. But still, something inside me said I had to try. Anything. Even if it killed me.

Which I knew it just might.

I told some friends that there was something I needed to do, and I was going to be gone for a while. I asked them to watch my kids for the day, and I got into my old '56 Chevy and started driving north. I drove and drove, not really sure of what it was that I was doing or what lay in store. I didn't have a plan. Not really. Just show up. That was my plan.

My mind relived that time over and over again as I drove. I tried to rewrite what had happened. Tried to make it so we decided not to stick around and keep my friend's wife company that night. I tried to imagine myself as stronger, able to say no instead of saying yes in the middle of the night and then again the next morning. But those were lies. That wasn't the real me. I was the one who had said yes. I was the one who had ruined my life and everyone else's.

I remember, as I drove, looking in the rearview window at a train in the distance behind me. The long train was running on a track parallel to the road I was driving down. I thought I was making good time, trying to keep the train behind me, but that beast of a machine caught up with my car, little by little. Ten minutes later, I was looking across the passenger seat at that massive Missouri Pacific engine right beside me. The engineer inside looked at me strangely out of his window. The Midwestern prairie was just beyond, stretching out for what seemed like forever. I tried to speed up, but the train did too. And coming down a hill, when I slowed down to let it pass, it slowed down and stayed right with me.

It was like time was standing still. Telling me something. Maybe that my past had caught up with me. That no matter how hard I'd try to ignore it or stay ahead of it, it was bound to catch up. To be with me. Like that locomotive, the past, it seemed, was bigger and more powerful than me.

At around seven p.m., I pulled into the little town where I'd heard my friend was now living and drove down the broken cobblestone streets until I found a phone booth. I looked up his name in the phone book and dropped a quarter in the slot. I dialed the number and listened to the ring. I could feel my heart beating out of my chest. He didn't answer.

His wife did.

"Can I talk to your husband?" I asked.

There was silence. A dozen years had gone by. Had she recognized my voice? *There's no way,* I thought. This was long before the days of cell phones and caller ID. Besides, I was on a pay phone. I wondered what was going through her mind.

"Sure," she said. "Hold on a minute."

I thought about hanging up, getting in my car, and getting the hell out of there. But I'd come so far. I was scared to stay on the end of the line but even more scared to hang up. I heard an old familiar voice say hello.

"It's me. Rory," I said, struggling to get words to come out. Silence again.

"Yeah, I know," he answered.

"I'd like to talk to you if I could," I told him. "I'm in your town. At a pay phone." More silence. And then even more.

"Ernie's," he said. "I'll be there in ten minutes." And then he hung up.

I looked across the downtown street from where I was standing on the corner, and nearby was a little beer joint with a sign above it that said Ernie's. The neon words *Cold Bud Light Sold Here* were blinking in the window just below. I walked in, found a seat at the bar, and ordered a Coke. There were only a half-dozen people inside . . . a couple in a booth, two guys shooting pool. My knees were shaking almost as bad as my hands.

What was gonna happen when he got there? I had no way to know. He hated me, and this was his chance to set me straight. Was he going to hit me? Probably. Maybe he'd bring a gun and shoot me. I hadn't thought about that. I didn't want to die. Yet I knew I deserved it, whatever happened. What if he asked me about that time? What was I gonna say? I couldn't change anything or make anything right. *This was a big mistake*, I thought. *I am an idiot. I should just leave.*

A thousand thoughts were running through my mind as I heard that front door open and I saw him walk in. Still handsome. Older now but strangely the same. The look on his face said he wasn't happy. He was gonna kill me. My heart started racing.

"Stand up," he said. I didn't move. I was frozen. My limbs had locked up.

"Stand up, I said," he repeated. This time a little louder. The two guys playing pool stopped and turned our way. This was it. I was a goner. I stood up and braced myself for what I knew was coming. But it never came. Instead, he did the one thing I never in a million years thought he would do.

He smiled.

And a tear came rolling down his cheek as he opened his arms and said, "I've missed you."

The man who should've killed me . . . hugged me instead. He put his arms around me and told me that he loved me.

I didn't know how to respond. What had just happened? How could he do this? Why wasn't he mad? Pissed off that I had stolen his wife and that part of his life from him? It didn't make any sense. But I soon realized why. He didn't hurt me because he was bigger than that. Because love, real love, is bigger than that. Bigger than hurt. Bigger than pain. Even bigger than fear. And somehow, he knew it.

No, he chose it.

Instead of punching me and cussing me out, he bought me a beer. He sat down on a barstool beside me and pulled out pictures of his kids. Those two little boys I had known years ago were handsome teenagers now, and in the pictures there were now a couple more kids too. He talked about how well he and his wife were doing, how he was helping coach their baseball teams, and how he'd been at the same job for quite a few years. And then he asked about my girls, Heidi and Hopie, and I pulled out my wallet and showed him pictures of them. I told him I had moved to Nashville and was writing songs. He was genuinely excited and proud for me.

He and I talked a long, long time. And he never once brought up what had happened back then or said one thing to make me think he was upset with me. Not one. As the evening wore on and he downed the last of a beer, he stood up and said he'd better be getting home, that he had to work in the morning. I grabbed his arm. I couldn't hold it back anymore. My tears started falling.

"I'm sorry," I said. "I'm so . . . so . . . sorry." I was sobbing now. I didn't care who saw. Maybe it was the beer. Probably not. It was, more than likely, guilt. And shame. Years and years of it, of carrying it around.

"I know you are," he said. And he hugged me again. "Me too," he said. "Me too."

And that was that. The unforgivable was forgiven.

That is the closest thing I know of to being able to understand what it means that Christ died for me. It was as if my sins had been wiped clean and I didn't have to carry them around anymore. The weight that had been so heavy was lifted. I still had the memories of what I did, the facts. But only as a reminder of what not to do in the future. Who not to be. And that part of it would be a good thing.

I drove back that night a changed man. I had witnessed something. Something from someone who was on a higher plane than what I was used to. I knew it was a moment I'd never forget. And I knew that I wanted to be like that. Like my friend from years ago, who is my friend still. To be able to face something that should make you angry and instead feel compassion. And love.

I didn't know it then, but I would someday have the woman I love taken from me. Against my will. And my family would be forever changed. I would have the chance then to choose to take a higher road too. To choose love and forgiveness instead of hate and anger, while a million people around the world watched. How I would deal with it, how I am dealing with it now. They would see something in me that was unusual and inspiring, I would learn later.

But the forgiveness and understanding that I have now came from my friend first. From God, ultimately, even before that. Yes, I have been forgiven greatly. Many times over. And so I must forgive greatly and trust that God has a greater plan in store than the one that I can see. I must remember that the story isn't over yet. It is still being written.

Day by day, scene by scene, moment by moment. As I am writing this story about my past, He is writing the story of my future.

And yours.

Fourteen

MARINE BIOLOGY

E leven weeks of basic training changed me. Forever.

How could it not? I'd never really been away from my mother or most of my siblings. Getting on that bus, then my first airplane, then another bus that led to the front gate of Parris Island—a legendary peninsula on the South Carolina coast where marines were either made or broken—the apron strings were ripped off mama's boys by screaming drill instructors who had stripes on their arms and fire in their eyes. The staff sergeant boarded the bus, then at the top of his lungs ordered us off, using profanities that struck immediate fear into the hearts of me and fifty other recruits with sleep in our eyes and peach-fuzz on our chins. It was clear: my childhood was over. Thank God.

I hated boot camp. And I loved it. Both at the same time. Probably the same way most boys have for the last two hundred years or so that the Marine Corps has been in existence. I was six feet two inches tall by then and skinny as a rail. One hundred and forty-four pounds. The recruiter said if I'd been a single pound less at my height, they wouldn't have let me in. Those eleven weeks, plus the next eight years of service to Uncle Sam, put some weight on me. Some muscle. And made me stronger in a thousand other ways too.

When I got out of boot camp, they flew me home. Back to Kentucky. My mom was at the airport to pick me up. I knew she was proud to see me in my short hair and uniform. We still didn't have a phone at home, so I had only been able to write letters. That made the separation even harder but better, probably. I was changed. I knew it. Mom did too. I remember walking through the airport, looking at all the families and lovers and children and feeling strange. Unable to understand how life for everyone else in the world had continued on the same while so much had changed for me. But it had.

Mom's old Duster was still running, barely. And she had a new boyfriend. So we headed to meet him at a truck stop on the Western Kentucky Parkway. I remember it was March, and it had started to snow—and then it happened. With the large Flying J sign a half mile ahead, Mom's car started to sputter, then shut down. I could hear the sound of a rod knocking, then a loud backfire as we steered the car onto the shoulder. Then we just sat there. Trying to figure out what to do next. I laugh about that day now, but I know we weren't laughing then. It was just another bit of hard luck in a life filled with nothing but bad luck for Mom. We walked the half mile through the snow to the truck stop and left the car there and never went back for it. Mom knew there was no way she could afford a towing bill, let alone the cost to fix it. So why bother? She just moved on and left that broken part of her in the past.

I did the same thing in a lot of ways. In the service I met guys from all over the country who were in the same boat I was and learned that there was a great big world out there, and I wanted to see it, to be a part of it. And soon I was. I spent a year in aviation electronic school at a naval base just north of Memphis, then was shipped out to California. Then to South Carolina, Japan, and even Kaneohe Bay, Hawaii, for my last couple of years. I worked on reconnaissance camera systems for F-4 jets and later F-18s. It was a good job, and I was pretty good at it. I excelled in the service, going from private to sergeant in only a few years.

Near the end of my four-year enlistment, I was offered the chance to reenlist. So I did. Not because I wanted to make a career of the marines but because I needed a new PA system to play music. Seriously. By then I was playing music in some clubs near the base in Beaufort, South Carolina, and needed new gear for the bigger places I was getting the chance to play.

That, and I was married by then and had a little one on the way. They offered me twenty-five thousand dollars to sign up for another four years, and I couldn't pass it up. It was more money than I or any of my people had ever seen before, and on top of it, I had no idea yet how I was going to get to Nashville and, if I did, how I would survive once I got there. That was 1985: it would still be ten years and two kids before my crooked path would lead me to Tennessee, where I wanted to be.

—∿—

I met my older daughters' mother in Garden Grove, California, in January 1985. I was stationed at El Toro and had a fake ID that some buddies and I had bought at a swap meet nearby. On weekends we would go to a little dance club for fun, and she was there one night. Pretty as a picture and sweet as could be, she was only eighteen and in her last year of high school. The next day I pulled my car into the drive-through at the Burger King where she was a shift manager. By the time she handed me a chicken sandwich and my change, she and I were pretty much inseparable. We were married that fall, and Uncle Sam shipped us to South Carolina soon after. We rented a nice house on Lady's Island, about ten miles from the base where I was stationed, and within a few months we learned she was pregnant.

Heidi Caroline was born in the fall of 1986. I remember that day like it was yesterday. Pacing the hall of Beaufort Memorial Hospital, waiting for news, and the doctor coming out the double doors, telling me that I had a daughter. I was elated. I had always loved the idea of having babies. Of being a father. So when Heidi came along, it was a magical moment for me. I couldn't get enough time with her. Her white-blond hair and soft blue eyes melted me and made me question what life was all about, what I was put on this earth for.

Unfortunately, her mom and I weren't doing well, and as time went on, I grew closer to the baby and further from the baby's mama. It's not that she did anything wrong; I was just empty still. I'd had a couple of relationships before she came along that weren't good ones, and I was restless and unhappy, I guess. Mostly unhappy with me. I would project that onto others for years to come before I finally came to realize that most of the problems in my relationships had to do with me and not the other person.

Sarah Hope was born almost two years later in the middle of a September night at Baptist Hospital in Memphis, Tennessee. We called her Hopie from the moment she took her first breath, and the name has been perfect for her. Filled with unwavering hope and joy and a childlike sense of naive wonder, she is exactly the opposite in many ways of her sister, who spends most of her days deep in thought, analyzing life to the nth degree. Heidi has always been the most like me, and Hopie is the most how I'd like to be. Together, they were my world, and I relished the time I had with them.

I had just returned from a six-month tour in Japan and was again stationed at the naval base outside of Memphis when Hopie was born. I was in the room helping her mom, trying not to faint, and found myself in complete awe of the miracle of childbirth. Hopie had long fingers and hands and immediately wrapped hers around mine with a strength that was very unlike a newborn. She is strong still. Physically and emotionally. It takes a lot to make Hopie cry, and she, at times, carries the weight of the world on her broad shoulders without anyone ever even knowing. She has always been solid as a rock in our family, and we would need a lot of stability in the years ahead.

In late 1988, when Hopie was just a few months old, we were transferred to the air station in Kaneohe Bay, Hawaii. I had always wanted to go there—who didn't?—and as we settled into base housing, I spent my off time playing sand volleyball and enjoying the sun and scenery. We all did. But the distance between the girls' mom and I had grown to a place where we could ignore it no longer. And soon she was on a plane headed to Jacksonville, Florida, to live with her mother and little brother. When she left, she took Hopie with her. Heidi stayed behind with me. I asked her to leave them both with me. I told her I would take the responsibility of them and she could start over with her life and have no ties to bind her. But in January of '90, I found myself at the American Airlines terminal in Honolulu with a three-year-old in my arms and her sister boarding a plane for a new life without us.

I wish I could tell you the girls' mother and I tried as hard as we could and that it just didn't work out. But that's not true. I was not a good man. I was unfaithful to her. And I was selfish and wanted more from life than the life we were building. In the end she, too, did some of the same things that I did and wasn't true to me. But I take complete blame for the failure of the marriage. I could've done more. Could've been more.

Time has had a way of making me realize that we can either lay the blame for our problems on someone else, letting that be an excuse for why our life isn't turning out the way we want it, *or* we can take the blame upon ourselves and let the responsibility for any change that should happen be on us. I don't harbor resentment or hold grudges against the girls' mom or anyone else. No one. It's not in me. Not anymore. It took a lot of years to get a good perspective, but now I see how freeing it is and how good it feels to be completely responsible for my actions. Good and bad.

Five months later I was in the same airport, boarding a plane to Florida to pick up Hopie and bring her back home. Her mom had decided it was too much for her, and a chance at a do-over was what she really wanted and needed. So I brought my eighteen-month-old daughter back to Hawaii and reunited her with her sister, and the three of us became a family unit for the next twelve years. Until Joey would walk into my life and theirs and show us once and for all what real love was. But, in the meantime, I had to continue trying to figure it out on my own.

Fifteen

FROM TEXAS TO TENNESSEE

O nce I was out of the service, we settled in Texas, where my mom and sister Marcy and older brothers were living. We lived with Marcy in a two-bedroom apartment for the first month or two. Me and the girls and the six members of my sister's family. It was hard, but it was also great fun. It was nice for my kids to be around their cousins and for me to be near my family too.

I thought it would be easy to get a good job with my experience in the service, but it wasn't. The Dallas market was flooded. So I started working temp jobs—sweeping floors and unloading boxes in a warehouse—and then realized I could make more money making music in the evenings. I found babysitters to keep the kids while I played in bars, and I picked them up at two or three a.m., my old PA system in the backseat still smelling of cigarette smoke and whiskey from the club. Some of my girls' favorite memories, even today, are of them waking up as I was pulling our car into the Whataburger drive-through in the middle of the night. Ordering a breakfast-on-a-bun for them and me to share and telling them all about my evening as they sat together in the passenger seat with one seat belt around the two of them as we drove into the dark night.

We found an apartment in the Las Colinas area, and Heidi soon started kindergarten. I played music five or six nights a week, from nine 'til one a.m., and sometimes two shows on Friday and Saturday nights, adding the one at a different bar, from five 'til eight p.m., then packing up and hightailing it to the later gig. Most of the time I hated playing those shows, where the bars were empty and I was playing to a lone bartender or one couple across the dance floor or a few drunks, talking and yelling over the songs I was singing. But it's where I cut my teeth, where I learned the craft of music. Of connecting with an audience, even when it's darn near impossible. And it's where the songs really got inside of me. I learned about writing great songs by singing great songs. It was an invaluable time for me as a musician and songwriter, and I look back on it with fondness now.

—⁂—

I drank too much. Slept with too many women. Made promises to some that I had no intention of keeping and I hated myself for it. But again, I didn't know any other way. When your heart is empty, you try to fill it up with whatever is handy. Whatever the culture tells you will make things better. Beer. Girls. Money. None of it helped. For a few hours it did, maybe, but it didn't last. It couldn't.

In between the shows, girls, alcohol, and kids, I made some trips to Nashville. I had met a couple of aspiring songwriters in the Dallas area and made the drive with them to Music City to see how my songs would stack up against the professionals. It was humbling, to say the least. The first couple of meetings were confusing. One person liked a certain thing about a song I played but hated the rest, and in the next meeting that person said the exact opposite. I soon came to realize that there is no right answer. I also learned that when you come across or write a great song, no one argues with that. I would arrive back in Dallas each time with a fire in my belly and a renewed goal of writing something extraordinary—something that no one could deny.

By the time the girls and I packed our things and finally moved to Nashville, it was the fall of 1994. The first month we stayed with a lawyer friend of a friend named Rod Phelps, then moved into an apartment on the west side of town in the community of Bellevue. It was a beautiful complex, very picturesque, with three pools and a big pond in the center. The girls and I thought we'd died and gone to heaven.

At first I got a job delivering flowers for a florist but found myself lost too often and not delivering the arrangements on time, so I moved on to waiting tables during the lunch shift at an Applebee's restaurant. But they had a thing called a "lightning lunch" that guaranteed that your lunch would be ordered and arrive back at your table within twelve minutes, or it was free. I bought a lot of free lunches in the month I worked there. I'm pretty sure the manager was glad to see me go. So was I.

We weren't making it, and I knew it, so we moved most of our stuff into a storage unit nearby and moved back to Texas for a while and lived out of our suitcases. An old girlfriend and I decided to make a go of it again, and that lasted exactly six months—until I loaded us back into our '56 Chevy and headed east for one more try in Nashville. It was September 1995. That would be the last move out of state we would ever make.

That old car was like a time machine for me. It somehow transported me to another day and time. To an era that I grew up hearing about from my father and had read about in books. It had no power steering and barely had any brakes at all, but I felt like somebody inside of it. The custom back license plate spelled out my name, RORYLEE, or at least most of it. *This town might not know who I am*, I thought as I drove it up and down Sixteenth Avenue, *but they're gonna know I'm here.*

Nashville quickly became home to us. I signed a publishing deal with the great Harlan Howard—a legendary writer who wrote Patsy Cline's "I Fall to Pieces," Buck Owens's "Tiger by the Tail," and hundreds of others—and was soon being paid to do what I love for a living. The contract I signed was for three hundred dollars a week with no raises, and it was a five-year deal. In the first year, I think I wrote 350 songs. Just about a new one every day. I would make a writing appointment with a different person every day; sometimes I'd make two. One in the morning and one in the afternoon. It would be three years and hundreds of songs that no one would ever hear before I would get my first song recorded.

Every night in the little apartment we lived in, I knelt beside Heidi's and Hopie's bunk beds, held their hands, and said a prayer with them. We would pray for a good night's rest and for our friends and family, but most of all we would pray for God to shine His light on one of my songs, to let it get recorded. We knew what that would mean and how much it could change our lives. We were living mostly on fish sticks, mac-and-cheese, and trips to Taco Bell's drive-through for a handful of thirty-nine-cent tacos. It was a wonderful life, but we hoped for more. We believed it was possible.

And it was. A song I had written—with a friend of mine named Tim Johnson—called "Someone You Used to Know," not only was recorded by a country artist named Collin Raye but also became a single and was played all over the radio and then hit number one on the Billboard charts. There must've been four hundred people at my first number-one party. I had made so many wonderful friends in Nashville. My mom drove in along with some aunts and uncles for the celebration. It was a big night for me. Bigger than I knew, actually. In a good way and a not-so-good way.

I had been dating a girl who was hell on me. And hell on my girls. We were on again, off again, and that night I think we broke up and got back together three times. She was excited for me and jealous and angry with me at the same time. After I got home and put the kids to bed, she and I were in the parking lot arguing. We both said some terrible things to each other, and out of anger, she took my car keys and drove off in her car. To show her who's boss, I found my extra set of keys and drove to a 7-Eleven and fished through my wallet for an old girlfriend's number and called her. The girl on the other end of the phone was more than excited to meet up and celebrate with a big number-one-hit songwriter, and so we did. When the sun came up the next morning, I was in that girl's arms in the backseat of my car, behind some building on Music Row.

I hated myself for being there. I hated who I was. I hated that I had let the greatest night of my life be ruined because of my own insecurities and then gone a step further and spent the night with someone I didn't care about. By the time I got home, everyone was waking up, excited to meet for breakfast and continue celebrating my accomplishment with me. As I sat with them in Cracker Barrel, hungover and looking like a zombie, I knew I had to do something. Had to change. Get my act together. But how?

Sixteen

SONG *RIGHTER*

I have said many times that I think I've spent too much of my life trying to write great songs and not enough time trying to be a great man.

It's true. I thought success would bring happiness, but it's the other way around. True joy and happiness have a way of attracting good things into your life. And if you aren't already happy when you find success, it will make you more unhappy. It will amplify what's already there. It did for me, anyway.

I had been going to church on and off for years. I'd joined and attended singles groups, and I'd even walked forward and given my life to Christ and been baptized. But nothing happened. I thought a brick would hit me in the head, and all of a sudden everything would be so much clearer and I'd be a different man. A better one. But it never happened, and I didn't understand why. I had started going to a Bible study on Sixteenth Avenue on Music Row a couple of years before, but I had mostly sat in the back—listening, reading, wondering if all this was really true. I wanted my life to change, but I didn't want to be turned into one of those boring, Goody Two-shoes Christian guys who I had met by the dozens. The ones who spoke of "being in the blood" and looked like they had never done anything wrong in their lives. I couldn't relate to them. Not in the least.

My world and my people were welfare and food stamps and cars that didn't run, and ex-wives and pain and sorrow. I felt like if I became a real Christian, I would be neutered. That all the real fun in life would go away. Yes, I would be more honest and a better man, but I'd be vanilla and plain and a nobody. I didn't want to be that. To others, I might have looked like someone who was successful, but inside I was still nobody—and that scared me.

So I kept doing things my way. Learning the hard way. Opening my hand a little at a time, trusting God with my life and my fears a little more, and a little more, until one day I found myself at a crossroad.

The money from my first hit song had bought the farmhouse we live in and royalties from the second had started fixing it up some. I was becoming a better man, little by little, and was feeling inspired by some fairly good choices I had made. But I was still struggling with giving absolute control of my life over to someone other than me . . . to Him. During this time, Mom was living in an RV across from our driveway (this was before it wouldn't run and would be permanently parked at a lot by the interstate a few miles from the farmhouse). The girls enjoyed having my mom in our lives, getting off the bus and sitting with her in lawn chairs while she smoked and told stories of the good old days, when their old man was young and the only cereal we had to eat was crumbled bread in a bowl with milk on it. And God was working on me.

I was dangerously close to turning it all over to Him, to surrendering everything once and for all. And I think the devil knew it too. I didn't know if the devil was real or not, but I knew the Bible talked about him being tossed out of heaven and having a pull on us, making us want to put ourselves first, to do sinful things, and that was something I could relate to. I could feel a fight going on inside of me, between good and evil. The promise of hope was battling with the truth of who I was inside . . . the me that no one really knew. They were fighting it out, and it was killing me.

Late one night I got in my car and headed up the interstate. Tears were falling down my cheeks, and I was crying out to God.

Part of me wanted to leave the old me behind and start walking a new path, no matter how scary it was. Another part of me was saying, *Let's just get out of here. You're just gonna screw those kids up because you're worthless. Let's get out of here!*

I drove to a big park and walked around. For hours and hours. It was late at night, and I hadn't told the kids or anyone that I was leaving or when I would be back. I just kept walking. And crying. And then I drove into downtown Nashville and walked those streets. I walked by the bus station where I had been during my first trip to Nashville, and I went in and sat down. Then I went to the counter and asked for a bus ticket. The lady at the counter said, "Where to?" I said, "Anywhere but here, lady." I boarded a Greyhound bus, and as it drove off, I stared out into the night. I imagined that I would end up at the ocean somewhere and would get a job on a boat, using a different name, keeping who I was a secret and starting a new life. One that didn't have the responsibilities I had. Didn't have the history or the emptiness. I could just be free. Invent a new identity and make a new life, leaving the old one behind.

But then I thought of my girls. What would happen to them? When they woke up and realized that I was gone and wasn't coming back? Would my mother raise them? Would they hate me? Or be better off without me? And I thought about God. This God who was supposed to come inside me if I asked for Him and fill me up so I wouldn't feel alone or so empty anymore. Where was this God? A million things went through my mind that night.

When I came to, the bus was in Louisville, Kentucky. Dropping off and picking up some more passengers. I got off and walked to the bathroom. Numb. Dead inside. I splashed some water on my face in a dirty sink and looked up. And then it happened. I saw him. Me. Him. God. Him in me. In the mirror. As I stood in the bathroom of that Greyhound station, I saw myself, and it suddenly occurred to me, for the first time, that maybe He was already there. Already in me. And all I had to do was believe it. I dried my hands, went to the counter, and bought another ticket, this time for home, then boarded a bus headed south for Nashville.

It was morning by the time I got to my truck and started heading to the house. I was driving down I-65, and the sun was rising over the buildings and the houses to the left of the interstate. I could feel something rising inside me too. I wasn't sure what it was, but it felt like hope. Real hope. In something greater. In something and Someone bigger than me. I knew I still had a lot to learn and would probably never completely figure out how this religion thing worked exactly, but I would choose to believe, and maybe that would be enough. Maybe. Just maybe.

And it was.

It still is. I can't say that today I understand much more about God's plan and how it all works than I did that morning while driving home from the bus station. I've never told this story before. Not to my kids or mother or anyone. I've always been embarrassed by it. But I've learned that most of the time, the things that you're most ashamed of and don't want to tell anyone are the things that can become a new beginning for you. And, in time, God has a way of making those moments the first things you want to talk about because it's from there that He was able to work in your life. To really change you. From the inside out.

And so, though I didn't understand it, I started just believing it. And if I really believed, wouldn't I act differently? So I did. And from acting differently, an amazing thing happened. Real change. Transformation. First in myself and then in everyone and everything around me. Nothing is the same. It is, but it isn't. After a while I didn't have to remind myself to make the good and right choices. I just started making them naturally. Because it felt so good.

Something happened to me. No, a brick didn't fall down from heaven, but it might as well have. I guess you could say I was saved. Or forgiven. Or born again. Whatever it was, it was powerful, and it was real. And it's made all the difference in my life.

Seventeen

BAGGAGE CLAIM

I did the best I could.

Just as I have with my mother and father, I have learned to forgive myself for the mistakes I made raising my older girls. I did the best I could with what I had. That's not really true, though, for me . . . I could've done better. Made better choices. But I didn't. Something inside kept me from making great decisions with my time, energy, and love, and that something was a part of me. So, in a way, the old me *couldn't* have done any better. He wasn't strong enough.

I forgive him. Me. I am disappointed in who I was. And I think about it and remember the mistakes I made and what they cost. Who they hurt. And I try, too, not to be like him.

I am me because of me. No one else. My decisions brought me here, good or bad. And my thoughts make up how I feel about myself and others and this life I live. I can choose to be negative, filled with regret. Or I can choose to be filled with hope. With life. A life of possibilities and wonder. Every day is a new day for me. A clean slate. I get to make what I want of it. It is a gift from God. The biggest gift, I think.

So I do not dwell on the past. Not ever. I don't blame anyone for who or what I've turned out to be, and I don't carry around my hurt or my baggage as excuses for how I got here. None of that matters to me. Today is all I care about. And tomorrow, of course. But today is what determines my tomorrow, and right here, right now is all I can really do anything about. So I stay in the moment—or I try to, anyway. It is a constant battle. Being present. Being completely present with the ones around you.

I can't tell you how many times my kids have told me at dinner or somewhere when we're spending time together, "You're not here, Dad. You're here, but not really." And they're right. My mind is on other things. A song. Or a movie script. Or a line in a book I've read. My mind is trying to multitask and thinks that it can do everything and please everyone. But it can't. You can't be here and be somewhere else at the same time. My kids know that it isn't a conscious thing that I do. It's not on purpose. I'm not trying to be distracted and have that blank stare in my eyes as they're talking to me. It's habit. Selfishness, I think. Putting my make-believe thoughts over what is real. What is in front of me. Putting myself above others. That is the bigger problem.

But at least I'm aware of it. And I'm working hard to change it. I've done better. The kids will tell you. Not just at that but other things too. Like being a father. Really being a father.

Eighteen

FATHER FIGURE

A s I think back on those earlier years, before God opened my eyes, I think I loved the idea of being a daddy the most. The truth is, it's tough figuring out how to be a good father when you don't have one around to emulate.

—᠁—

As I mentioned earlier, I have a way of putting a blurred or romantic lens on things that are hard. It's a good thing in some ways, but it can also block out parts of reality that need to be there. Like putting your kids' education above the romantic idea of them just going to school where the bus picks them up in front of the house . . . the way it was done when I was young. That's a fine idea, but we are deep into a whole new century since the one I was in as a boy, and things are different now. The world is different, and all schools are not equal. I should've put my girls in the school that would've given them the best education and experience to grow. I could have. But I didn't, and they suffered for it. Hopie especially.

And I wasn't good with money either, so we lived in fear a lot of the time. Fear of what going to a doctor would cost, so we didn't go. We never had insurance when my kids were growing up, so unless it was life-threatening, we just didn't go to the doctor. Being sick wasn't allowed because we couldn't afford it. Seriously. I never said it out loud, but the kids knew that was how we lived. And that's fine for a thirty-year-old man, but not for a four-year-old with a cough that won't go away. Or a seven-year-old who fell off her bike and hurt her shoulder badly. I just iced it and said it was gonna be okay. And it was. Heidi's broken collarbone healed in time, but it left a scar that she and I both still see and some scars that we can't.

Another time she broke her leg on the playground when she was five, and I called the ask-a-nurse hotline. I was told to check and see if it was swelling or if she was running a fever, and she wasn't, so I figured she was probably okay. So for the next twenty-four hours, I carried her with me to set up my equipment at a gig I was playing and everywhere else I went that day. She just had to grin and bear it. And she did.

When I finally took her to an ER, an X-ray of her leg was done, and the doctor took me out of the room and showed me the scan. The bone was broken completely in two. "This little girl's in a lot of pain," he said. I looked at the fracture, and tears poured down my face. Partly because I realized how much pain Heidi had been in for the last twenty-four hours and partly because I hated living that way. Hated that I couldn't provide better for them.

Heidi wore a cast for the next four or five weeks, and then I managed to do what I always did. Skip out on the bill. We moved, or I stayed one step ahead of the billing address I had given and never paid for the cast. I could have. Plenty of people put themselves on a budget, setting money aside to pay a little something each month of what they owe to someone. But that's not how I thought. Not who I was. I was still many years away from learning the joy of "doing the right thing."

And it wasn't just with them. It was with me too. I broke my ankle one afternoon when I left the car running and ran in to get something from the apartment. As I came back out the door, I saw that the car had started to roll down the hill. I jumped completely off a fifteen-foot landing to try to get to it and broke my left ankle in the process. I heard it snap and tried to crawl after the car. Luckily, one of my neighbors jumped in and put the brake on before it could pick up any speed. I got lucky that day with the car but not my ankle. Like the kids, I just had to deal with it. And so I did. In time, it healed and got better.

I was the same way with taxes. We didn't make much money most of the time, and I definitely didn't want Uncle Sam to take a bunch of what already wasn't really enough to live on—so I just stopped paying taxes. Stopped turning in my yearly tax returns. For eight years I didn't turn in a single one. By then, I had started making good money writing hit songs and was doing pretty well, but I was still afraid that I might never see any more money and avoided paying taxes altogether. The tax man never came to get me, but Joey sure straightened me out that first year we were married when she found out I owed forty-two grand to the IRS.

I read a book one time that said some people live with a "scarcity outlook" on life, believing there is only so much to go around, and if they don't fight for what's theirs, they won't get any. And if they don't hold on to it, it will go away, and there won't be any more to get. I was like that. Always believing there wasn't enough. And there wouldn't be. But the book also said that some people live with an "abundance outlook." This is how I see life now: there is always enough to go around. More than enough. And the best way to have more is to give what you have now away. It doesn't make any sense, but it works. The other way, the way I was living before—out of fear—made complete sense to me then. But that way does not work.

Nineteen

DUCT-TAPE PARENTING

One man, two daughters, and a roll of duct tape. What could go wrong?

She kept pulling her feet off the pedals—scared that she would lose her balance and fall off her bike. I had to use the duct tape. How else could she have learned to ride?

It's true. Sad, yes, but true. When Heidi (and later Hopie) was learning to ride a bicycle, I duct-taped her feet to the pedals of her little pink Huffy. After doing what she'd asked and removing her training wheels earlier that day, I had spent the morning running beside her, up and down the block, as she tried to find the courage to ride like a big girl. I kept telling her to keep her head up, to just watch the sidewalk in front of her, but she would get scared and look down and take her feet off the pedals to stop the bike. So, in true dad fashion, I fixed it.

I had the solution in a toolbox in the trunk of my car. A roll of gray duct tape.

But sometimes the solution is also the problem.

Heidi did learn to ride her bike that day, and so did Hopie a few months later. But it came at a cost. You can't force someone to be brave. To have the courage needed to face their fears. It's gotta come from inside them, when they're ready—not when *you're* ready for them to be ready. I didn't know that. I was a man who had to be more than just their father. I had to be their mother too. At times, I did pretty well walking that line.

91

Being both. But sometimes, like with the duct-tape incident, I will go down in history as being not only a crappy substitute mother but also a crappy father.

My kids laugh about it now. They love to hear me tell that story. They think it's hilarious. Never mind that as a grown-up Heidi won't go near a bicycle, and Hopie stays clear of anything that resembles duct tape. It is a funny story, though. In hindsight, especially.

Unfortunately, that wasn't the first or only time I used duct tape to solve a problem with the kids. When Heidi was about a year and a half, she would habitually run her right hand through her hair (like her daddy did) when she was sucking her thumb (which her daddy didn't do), and each time she did, some of her silky-soft blond hair would come out in her fingers. We tried to break her of the habit, but we couldn't. Pretty soon, there was a big bald spot in the back right side of her hair, and we had a problem that needed a solution.

Duct tape.

We bought her a little blue Cookie Monster mitten at Kmart, and I duct-taped it to her right hand. That way, when she tried to run her fingers through her hair, none came out. Great. Problem solved. In a month or two her hair had grown back, and we were able to throw the now-filthy glove away. But something bigger than that had been set in motion: my belief that a temporary solution could solve a permanent problem. But it can't.

Twenty

SELF-HELP WAS NO HELP

I came to learn that what I had was a character problem. I wanted the benefits of being a man with good character, without having to change and actually have that character.

I wanted a quick fix. We all do, I guess. A book about real change that I could thumb through quickly while reclining on a lawn chair at the swimming pool at our apartment complex, drinking a wine cooler, and listening to George Strait on my Sony Walkman. While the kids played Marco Polo in the shallow end, I could figure out my deeper problems and head home a few hours later with the same old wet towels and a new-and-improved me.

I bought lots of books written by lots of big self-improvement gurus, such as Tony Robbins, Stephen Covey, and Norman Vincent Peale, with lots of titles that sounded great: *The 7 Habits of Highly Effective People* and *The Power of Positive Thinking*. The truth is, I loved those books. They were inspiring. I would highlight lines or paragraphs I'd read and say them over and over again to myself. Yet nothing ever changed. I would come in from a hard day of reading at the pool, take a shower, and look in the mirror and still see the same guy I was before. I didn't understand it.

This would go on for a long time. Trying to jump-start change, but nothing ever happening. Maybe some small things. Noticeable to me, but not to anyone else. Things that didn't last. It was like carrying around a big roll of duct tape for my life, and every time I saw something that was wrong or falling apart, I just ripped off a piece and prayed that it would hold. But it wouldn't. It can't. That's not how real change happens.

I would do the same thing a number of years later with Christian books too. It was a new phase with different authors—C. S. Lewis, Max Lucado, Rick Warren—and the titles were different too: *The Purpose Driven Life* or *I Really Want to Change . . . So, Help Me God.* The results, however, were the same. It was the old swimming-pool philosophy, only with a different set of books. I wanted change to happen without making any real changes. This time, instead of teaching or tricking my brain to do it, I was going to trick my heart, using prayer and God.

Honestly, for years, I didn't understand why it wasn't working. I was doing everything they said to do. Trying to follow the step-by-step process to a better me and a better life. But the results were the same; only the section at the bookstore was different.

Twenty-One

DIE LIVING

My mother smoked her whole life. She took her first puff around age thirteen, and she took her last at seventy-one.

A Winston was still burning in the ashtray next to her recliner when she took her last breath in July 2014. Like most people, she tried to quit a few times, but it was too hard. When you start anything that young, it's tough to walk away from it. She finally did quit smoking though . . . when her heart quit beating.

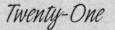

Mom was diagnosed in 2005. My sisters and I went with her to her appointment at Vanderbilt, and we listened to the doctor tell her that it was because of the cigarettes. She was upset about that. Upset mostly that we were in the room to hear it. That the doctor confirmed what we had always told her might happen if she didn't quit those nasty things. She knew the truth of it, but I don't think she wanted us to know what caused that spot on her tongue. She wanted to keep it vague, like it was just one of those things that happen to people sometimes. Bad luck. Dr. Sinard could tell it made her uncomfortable and that she wanted to gloss over it, so he said it again: "Those cigarettes are gonna kill you, Mrs. Feek, if you don't stop."

And he was right. They did.

Those and the beer and the hurt and the pain. And old age. Who knows what actually causes a heart to stop beating when it finally does. It could've been one or all of those things, truthfully, or something else, I guess. But we didn't need an autopsy to tell us what took our mother from us.

Cancer.

It wasn't the first time that word had crept into our family's vocabulary and, unfortunately, wouldn't be the last. My youngest sister, Candy, had breast cancer in her early thirties, and she had come out of the surgery, chemo, and radiation fine and was still doing well. But this was different. Less random and more scary for some reason. I don't know why.

Maybe it was Mom's age—mid-sixties by then. Or maybe it was her years of hard living. Whatever it was, it got her attention and ours.

After a brutal surgery—going through Mom's neck to take half of her tongue, using flesh from her arm to fix her neck and skin from her leg to fix her arm—Mom was left with scars in all three places and speech that would be forever slurred. She was self-conscious about it. About being hard to understand. But she learned to embrace it in the end. Her lisp became a kind of battle scar from her war with the cancer that had tried to take her down.

When she came home from the hospital after a week in intensive care, she followed the doctor's orders and quit. For six months she stayed clear of her smokes. Alcohol too. My sisters scrubbed her little brick HUD house from floor to ceiling to try to remove the smell of nicotine so she wouldn't be tempted when she got home. And it helped. For a while.

To make it easier, my brothers quit too. Or at least in the waiting room, during her surgery, they swore they would. I know they wanted to quit, but instead they just hid their smokes when they came to visit Mom and walked outside to do their smoking away from her. They could see her scars and knew what the cancer had put her through, but as scary as that was, it was no match for the years and years of having a shot of nicotine in-between their fingers when they were nervous or had finished eating or whenever.

After six months, Mom sent my brother to the store for a pack, and she started back up. Beer and wine magically started showing up again in her fridge too. At first it upset me. Upset my sisters. But we learned to accept that this was her life, and she had the right to make her own decisions about how to live it. But she never smoked in the house again. Sort of. She loved the way her house smelled after the girls cleaned it and wanted to keep it that way. So she went outside to smoke. Until it turned winter and that became too inconvenient and she just cracked open a window in the laundry room, put a fan in to blow the smoke out, and lit up. It seemed the same as smoking inside to me, but for her it was change, and real change was hard for her to come by. So we all were thankful for it, no matter how small it was.

It was January 2014 when we heard the word *cancer* again. Mom called each of us on her cell phone from a waiting room at the community hospital in Columbia and said, "You might want to come down here." She didn't say why. She didn't have to. We knew.

She had gone in that morning for a scan to see why she was having a hard time swallowing. Her throat had been bothering her for a while, and she thought it might have been acid reflux causing it. That's what she hoped, anyway. But inside, she probably knew or suspected what it was. When we got to the hospital, the doctor showed us the scan and explained that the mass on her esophagus was a squamous cell carcinoma. Esophageal cancer. And they were pretty sure there were some spots on her lungs too. We knew enough about cancer to know that when it returns, it isn't a good thing. Mom did too. There was a good chance that this one was going to leave more than just a scar.

We went with her a few days later to see an oncologist. That didn't go well. He was blunt. He brought up her smoking again. This time Mom wasn't going to put up with it. She was mortified and felt disrespected and demanded to see a different doctor. So we arranged for her to have another oncologist, and this one took a softer approach. She needed the cancer to be random and not related to the cigarettes, so we all just played along. My brothers vowed to quit smoking again, then doubled the number of packs they smoked a day. It was heartbreaking for all of us, and stressful. My sisters, though, were amazing. So loving and patient with Mom through all of the meetings and scans and opinions on how to treat it. Then Mom told us she had decided on a plan.

She was going to do nothing.

She had no plans to quit smoking again or to stop drinking or anything else. Her time had come, and she knew it. She was going to live. That was her choice, and we all knew that she would most likely not live long, but it was her choice, and she was going to do nothing.

We were outraged. We demanded that she fight. The doctors said she had a decent chance of surviving if they did the big surgery, where they remove the esophagus and stretch the stomach up to your throat—if she lived through it, that is. But it was a chance. We thought she was being weak. Giving up too soon. All so she didn't have to quit smoking. *Dang, I hate those cigarettes!* I said to myself for the thousandth time.

But I was wrong. That wasn't the case. She wasn't quitting or being weak. Over the next six months she would show us, and everyone around us, what it meant to be strong. To have courage. To live. And to die. The way you want. On your own terms. It was incredible.

Mom was living at that time in a little white-frame house, just down the road from us, that Joey and I had purchased for her a few years earlier. That house is one of the things I am most proud of—to have been able to do something for her. Truly do something that she couldn't have done on her own. She loved that house. It's the only one she ever owned. The only piece of land that was actually hers. And she was so proud of it. She planted roses and moonflowers all around and spent her days watering and weeding and sitting under her big covered patio, with a cigarette in her hand and her children and grandchildren all around her.

She also loved her neighbors. She brought them flowers and meals and called them daily, and they all loved her. That little house was more than a house. She finally had a home of her own. Even if it was for only a short while.

A month or two after her diagnosis, hospice came in. And she mothered and loved each of them. As the ladies from hospice checked on her, my mother checked on them and always left them feeling better about themselves than when they came. As her health declined, her joy increased. She loved life—what was left of it. She truly loved it and lived it to the max. That spring and early summer, my brothers and sisters and I were at her house constantly. We spent every Sunday having brunch together, grilling out and laughing and gardening and listening to her stories. It was strangely beautiful. Her dying and it giving her grown kids the chance to really live. Together.

I had no idea at the time how important Mom's death would be. Not to me but to my wife. How Joey seeing her mother-in-law be so strong in facing the unknown would help her in her own journey a year and a half later.

But for that time, it just felt good. It felt right.

Aunt Mary came to live with my mother that summer. For almost two months she stayed with her and kept her company and loved on her. After all those years of Mom being at her house, Aunt Mary knew how important my mom was to her and wanted to be there for and with her, in her time of need. And she was incredible. It was Aunt Mary on the other end of the line when I got the call early one morning that July: "Rory," she said, "you need to get down here."

Since Mom's house was only a mile or so from mine, I was there in no time. I found my mother in the laundry room. Fan running. Cigarette burning. She was struggling to breathe but still forcing a smile when she saw me and my siblings. We put our arms around her and told her how much we loved her. We did. We all did. And I think she knew it. Within an hour or so, Mom would pass and a shell of herself would be left in the chair. Mom's body was still there, but she was gone. That was clear to me.

I hadn't been around death much. Not at all, really. I had seen my wife's beloved dog, Rufus, pass away a few years before and had experienced his spirit leaving his body when the vet gave him the shot that would relieve him of unbearable arthritic pain. I saw his eyes a moment before, and then after. He was gone. It was the weirdest thing. I didn't really know what to make of it then. And I didn't know how to feel about it as I sat beside my mother, her hand growing colder as the time passed. Strangely, it was the same.

My sister Marcy lost it. Completely. She wouldn't find it again for almost a year. She was completely unprepared for the loss she would feel. No medications or midnight trips to the emergency room or even trips out west to weekend grief retreats would help her. Only time would.

When I had stood over my father's casket at his funeral, I didn't know what to do. But there at Mom's house, I did. When the men from the funeral home came, I told them I wanted to pick her up and put her on the linen-covered stretcher that would wheel her to the long vehicle that would take her away. I wasn't afraid or nervous. It felt natural. This was my mother, for God's sake. She had picked me up and held me in her arms the day I was born. I could hold her in mine the day she left us.

There is another family that lives in my mother's white-frame house now. I try not to be hateful to them, in my mind, when I drive by, but sometimes I am. It bothers me to see their cars parked in Mom's driveway—one of them up on blocks in the carport that she loved. To see the clutter on the front porch and in the yard that she loved so much. But, in another way, I recognize that this is life. That it's beautiful. My sister Marcy already had ripped up every flower and bush that Mom had and replanted them at her house. These people now have dozens more growing. Beautiful flowers and roses everywhere. Mom would love seeing them. And it clearly looks like life is going on there. Lots of it.

As it should be.

Twenty-Two

NEVER GONNA HAPPEN

I remember it too well. I wish I didn't, but I do.

It was the spring of 2000, and my green Expedition was parked in the driveway of our farmhouse. Heidi was sitting in the passenger seat, and Hopie was in the back. I was explaining to them that I was getting back together with the girl I had been dating. Again. Although I had told them the last time was the last time, I explained that I had changed my mind and had decided to try to make a go of it again. To make it work.

Heidi started sobbing. So did Hopie. They were upset and rightly so. They didn't trust the girl I was dating, and, even more so, they didn't like how she treated me—how much she had hurt their father. It's not that she was a bad woman; she was just bad for me. Like so many other girls I had dated before her, there had been a physical chemistry between us but no magic when it came to the heart. But I had once again resolved to make it work. I was tired of failing at relationships and had poured a year and a half, on and off, into this one. I was bound and determined to turn it into something good or die trying.

The kids were beside themselves. They had been drug through many relationships since their mother had moved on from our lives. And though none of them were great, this one had been especially hard on us. With tears in her eyes, Heidi begged me not to get back together with her. She knew it wasn't good and, different from me, she knew why.

Wiping the hurt that was rolling down her cheeks, she said, "Don't you see it, Dad? Everyone knows you deserve something great, to be with someone special. Everyone knows it, Dad. Everybody but you."

It broke my heart to break my girls' hearts. But I couldn't help it. I was too wounded. Too lonely. Unable to make the right decision. I listened, and then, against my daughters' wishes, I got back together with the girl. And as they suspected, and I did, too, it didn't last. We broke up again, one final final final time a few weeks later.

I was devastated. Emptier than empty.

Sometimes rock bottom is the place for us to be. Usually, though, we just don't seem to recognize the bottom, and we keep digging ourselves deeper and deeper into a hole that's going nowhere. Until one day, tired and exhausted, we give up. And start trying to climb out.

I would have to learn the hard way, again and again, before I would actually ever really learn anything. I was stubborn. Prideful. And God needed me to get all of that out of my system before He could really work in my life. And when I finally did, a funny thing happened. Not only did I change, so did everyone around me.

Twenty-Three

A NEW FAMILY

Sometime after my mother and brothers and sisters moved to Tennessee, I saw my family do an about-face. They were different. Kinder. Better. The funny thing is, though, the only one who really did any changing at the time was me.

My family had always been fractured. Hurt. Wounded. Struggling to be something better than it was. Something beautiful.

There were times through the years, after we were grown, when we got back together—but a distance remained. It still does now, in some ways. But it's better. Much better. I've learned to love my family for more reasons than the common Irish blood that runs through our veins. Warts and all. And, even more so, they have learned to love me.

—⁓—

By the time my family started moving to Tennessee in late 1999, God had been working on my character for a year or so. Teaching me patience and love and honor. Things that, at the core, didn't come easy for me. But as I changed, as I softened, so did they. I almost didn't recognize my mom and brothers and sisters. I thought I had woken up into a different family than the one I was born into. A good family. One that really, truly cares about one another.

I learned a lesson in that. After years of thinking that the problem was them, I realized that it was actually me. Not necessarily in an "it's all my fault" sort of way, but more in a "be the change you want to see" way. I don't know what happened. But if I do the math, that's how it adds up. We became more of a family when I became more of a man. But I couldn't fix all of it. It's about all of our journeys. About the good *and* the bad. Our lives together never stayed just one way or the other. They were always evolving. Changing.

Not too long after we became close, we got fractured again and hardly spoke. Someone teed someone off (probably me), or somebody hurt someone's feelings or got in somebody's business or asked about something they weren't allowed to ask about . . . and we grew apart. But then, over time, we found ourselves back together. I've come to realize that we're never going to get it figured out. We're not going to come to our senses and be the family I want us to be. We're just going to be us. And that's okay. Life is complicated, and family is even more complicated. I am learning to embrace it for what it is and not dwell on what it's not. To love even the slightest bit of headway we make, to celebrate the small victories and not worry about the war. To laugh at the insanity that it is sometimes, instead of letting it drive me crazy.

I think this mind-set has made it easier for me to love all my siblings. And, even more so, it has made it easier for them to love me. I have to constantly tell myself, "They're doing the best they can with what they have," and I have a feeling they are at their houses right now, thinking of me, saying, "He's doing the best he can with what he has."

I love that.

Twenty-Four

CIRCA 1870

The house was built in the 1870s. Restoration on it began in 1999, right about the same time it began in my heart.

It was summer, and I was house hunting. It was my first time looking for a house to buy. My people usually go through their whole lives and never buy a house, but I knew that before too long I was probably going to be able to afford one. As I mentioned earlier, a song I had written became a big hit on the radio, and the royalties all began magically to add up and, within a month or two, turned into a six-figure check that I received in the mail. And then another smaller one.

I looked at only three houses, really two, before I bought the one we live in now. I guess I wasn't a very smart shopper. I only had one real thing I was looking for. *Old.* That was it. Ideally, I think I wanted it to be a farmhouse. I had no idea why really. I had been living in the city pretty much my whole adult life. The kids and I were in a really nice apartment complex outside of Nashville, and they were going into fourth and sixth grades. A house in a subdivision made more sense, and something new or nice made even more sense. I had no idea how to fix up an old house. Even if I knew how, I didn't have the tools.

But that day as I drove down Highway 431, around a curve, and saw the homemade For Sale sign at the end of the driveway, I took note and wrote down the number on a little scrap of paper. It looked like an old place. Pretty big, too, white with barns around it. I drove on since I was on my way to look at a house in a little town called Lewisburg, about fifty miles south of Nashville. The picture in the ad that I had seen was of an older white gingerbread-looking house on five acres. When I got there, I realized it was practically brand-new. Made to look old. I just backed out of the driveway. Didn't even walk up to it. Instead, I drove to a phone and called the number on the scrap piece of paper.

"Thirty acres and the house for a hundred and sixty thousand," the man said. More or less. I could buy more land around it if I wanted or as little as five acres. He said the house was pretty run-down, built around 1870, and the family that was living in it had been there since the mid-1930s. I hung up the phone and drove straight to the house.

Harold Blaylock came to the door. Pulling his overall straps up, he shook my hand. He had a Chapel Hill Air Conditioning and Funeral Home farmer's cap on. He invited me to meet his wife, Joy, and then drove me around the property in his old pickup truck. I liked him immediately. He said they'd been there since he was ten years old, but due to his wife's ailing health, they were gonna need to move into town. They were hoping it would go to someone nice, who would appreciate what it meant to them and the families who'd lived in it before.

By the time I shook his hand good-bye, it was also to say, "It's a deal." Harold and his sister Reba financed me, and I gave them the down payment a couple of weeks later. They moved out that weekend, and the kids and I started working on it while they were still moving boxes into their truck and trailer. It was pretty rough living for the girls and me the first couple of years, but gradually it got better. Nicer.

I took a friend of mine who was a carpenter through the house to look at it not long after I bought it. We stood on the front porch afterward, and when I said, "Isn't it something?" he looked at me like I was crazy and said, "You got bigger cojones than I do, son." I didn't know what he meant.

"Do you know how much time and money it's gonna take to fix this place up?" he asked. I didn't. And I actually didn't have a clue. Then he said, "I would never do it. I wish I could, but it would be too scary." And then he patted me on the back and added, "But you gotta gamble big if you want to win big." Before he left, he told me that if I stuck it out, the house would be an amazing place to raise my kids and pass on to them when I'm gone. And he was right. It is.

There were times I wanted to sell it. Or burn it down. And just take off running for Nashville or somewhere easier. Closer to my friends and to the world and the people I knew. But I kept thinking about what he had said, so I stayed and continued working on it. Even when I didn't want to, I stayed. And for two years, pretty much all I did was work on the house, fixing it up.

What I didn't realize was that God had given me the house so that as I was working on it, He could work on me. I spent countless hours and days by myself, painting and caulking and hanging drywall and plumbing and a million other things that needed fixing. All the while, I think, God was fixing me. Healing parts of me that were broken. As the house began to come back to life, so did I. And it happened without me even realizing it. Much like the house, my changes were subtle. I would be working on one part of the house, making little improvements, constantly aware of the huge list of things left to do and not really seeing that the place was becoming beautiful. Unrecognizable, in a good way, to the neighbors around us. That's how my character was changing too. I saw a long list of things that still needed to be worked on, but people began to see the stuff that had been restored. Made new again.

Both the house and I were well on our way, but we would need more than just the tools I had to complete the job. It was going to take a woman's touch to make the house a home, but God wasn't going to let that happen until I had done my part and the house was ready. And He wasn't going to bring love my way until He knew my heart was where it needed to be too.

Twenty-Five

SOMETHING GOOD

I just wanted a little bit of something good. What I got was a lifetime of something great.

It didn't have to be amazing or beautiful. It could just be okay. And that would have been enough. I got down on my knees in the spring of 2001 and asked God to let me experience love that wasn't terrible. That's all I asked for.

But what He gave me was beyond my wildest, wildest dreams.

—⁂—

After years of longing for and never really having or feeling love, I got on my knees one final time and turned it over to God. Everything. All of it. I opened that last little bit of my hands and humbled myself and emptied myself to Him. And then I rose to my feet and tried not to be the man I had been for the last thirty-five years. If I was ever gonna have something different, I would have to make different decisions. And so I did. Or at least really tried to.

I began really searching my heart to see what my intentions were for everything. To question my own integrity even when no one else did. To expect more of myself because I knew I was capable of it and I was tired of living life empty and alone. Little by little, the world moved. At first it was so slight that I hardly noticed. I would find myself asking, "How are you doing?" when I would see someone, and really meaning the question, instead of just saying hello. And people could tell that I meant it, and they would answer by actually telling me how they were doing. Telling me things they never would've before. I would humble myself and ask, "What does that mean?" when someone used a word I didn't understand. I tried to be the reverse of my old self. Partly because I didn't trust myself and the decisions I had made but also because I wanted to see where a completely different path would lead me. I didn't just say, "Jesus, come into my heart and change me." I took responsibility for it and did my part.

But mostly, I repented.

I never used to like that word. I don't really like church words, like *repent* and *born again*, and, honestly, a hundred others that you hear a lot of Christians use in conversation. I always felt like they were showy and big—words meant to impress the listener, rather than the speaker being sincere. So I avoided them. I still do, except for *repent*. I've learned to really love that word. It's where the change is. And where the power is, in my opinion.

It's not enough to say I'm sorry. I believe that you have to show it. And *repent* is a biblical word for meaning what you say, then putting your money where your mouth is. My cousin Aaron told me a story about how, when he became a Christian, the church he was attending in Illinois at the time required him to have a time of repentance. He had to go back to everyone he had wronged and apologize to them, to try to make amends for the mistakes he'd made. That was scary stuff, he said, but in another way, he loved it. And it worked. It took him six months, but when it was done, he was a completely different person or on his way to becoming one.

I could see why. That was crazy-talk. My first reaction was of terror, but on second thought I could see how magic could come from it. I had a feeling that that kind of making amends would be so humbling to the person who was doing it, that change was bound to happen. It was almost forcing you into another life because you were blowing your old one wide open. That terrified but excited me at the same time. I had seen the change it had made in Aaron's life and in others' lives, and I desperately wanted to do whatever it would take to be the man I knew I needed to be. The man God wanted me to be. So I went for it.

I picked up my phone and called old girlfriends and told them how sorry I was for hurting them. They were shocked and probably skeptical. I can't blame them. But it was real. I really was sorry. And I really did want to change. I did my best to face up to everyone and everything that I had been hiding from and scared of in my past. And as frightening as it was, it was so much more rewarding to do. Humility is always a good thing. I've come to learn that you can never lose if your intention is to humble yourself and put others first. There is no downside. Not one.

And it wasn't for only six months; I'm still doing it. Or trying to. To apologize right away when my ego takes off running and leaves God and others in the dust. I'm still trying to remember that this life really isn't about me, no matter how many times the man in the mirror tells me it is. That serving is always better than being served. Giving better than receiving. And that love is always the best choice. Sometimes I get it right, right away. And at other times, I still have to learn the hard way.

Twenty-Six

FARMER BOY

I like to tell people that I might not have deep pockets, but I sure got a lot of them.

I'm not sure why, exactly, or even when I started wearing bib overalls all the time, but around the time I bought the farmhouse, I started wearing them a lot. Maybe it was because they were so comfortable or because I had spent eight years in the Marines and something about the overalls reminded me of a uniform. Or maybe it's just one less thing to worry about. I'm not really sure. I just started wearing them and never stopped.

For the last ten or fifteen years, I've pretty much worn nothing else. Just bibs. And I've got all kinds. Dark blue, light blue, black, white, tan-colored, striped, you name it; I've got it. Or had it. Some are blue-jean bibs for daily wear, some are heavy-duty cotton that can hold off a pretty extreme amount of cold, and some are super lightweight custom bibs that Carhartt made for me for summertime last year. I've got lots of Carhartts and some Keys, a few Libertys, and even some Big Smiths, but they're all pretty much the same. They're built mostly for work and for comfort, not for looks. The funny thing is, though, the way they look has made a big difference in our lives. They're part of why a lot of people know who we are. I guess my wife and I are just easy to spot. The guy in the overalls with the pretty girl. That's us in a nutshell.

They call it branding. I call it lucky. Sorta like what Forrest Gump might say about his running: "I just started wearing them . . . I had no idea they would take me anywhere." But they have. In a world of singers and performers who look the same, my overalls are part of what makes Joey and me look different.

I myself like them for a different reason, though. I like them for all the men who've worn them over the years. Mostly farmers. Farmers, factory workers, and other working types. In the history books you'll see scores of men wearing them in photos from the Great Depression and before. All of them doing hard labor. Doing jobs no one else wants to do. Work that doesn't get much pay, and even less glory.

Men like Joe Farlow. He's my neighbor down the road. He and his Shirley have been living in the same little house for sixty-something years. He farmed and did a number of other things, but he's long retired now. I mostly see him these days when he's walking out to get his mail from the rusted white box by the road and I'm passing by. Just a wisp of the man he once was, but he's still wearing bibs. Joe probably weighs less than a hundred pounds soaking wet, but he is one of thousands, millions, who've worn them their whole lives. They never knew any different or wanted to. They weren't trying to make a fashion statement. They were just getting dressed to do the job that was waiting for them in the barns and the fields, sitting on red and green tractors or on stools beside milk cows.

I also have loved wearing them because they're pretty much a natural girl repellent. The whole time I was married, I don't really remember any women looking my way or giving me much of a second thought. I liked knowing that. I'm guessing Joey did too. "One less thing," I would always say. One less very important thing, actually.

But my wife thought I was handsome in them, and that's all that really matters. She looked at me the way a man wants his wife to look at him. And I know that she knew that she was the only one I was ever really trying to impress anyway. So that was nice. It always feels good to do the best right thing. And that was one of them for me.

I have my moments these days when I think about wearing something else. Some jeans or shorts. And I will sometimes, mostly around the house or working outside. Who knows? I might even decide to start wearing jeans again full-time, one of these days. Or khakis or something else. Just because I can. And also because I don't want to be defined by something on the outside. I'd rather be known for what's inside of me. The man that I am, not the man that I *look* like I am.

But for now, I'll just buckle up my straps and keep working—if that's what typing on the computer is. A gentleman farmer. That's what someone called me one time. The kind who writes more about sitting on the horses in the pasture than actually sitting on them. I'm working on that, though. Putting down the pen and picking up the reins more. Spending more time living life and less time writing about living. That is part of what my wife helped me to do. Helped me stay balanced. I am having to learn it on my own now, and it's not easy.

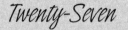

KILLING MYSELF

I t was my first truly unselfish act. The first one of any substance that I can remember. And nothing came of it. Nothing, except everything, that is.

It was January or February 2001, and my sister Marcy was living here in Tennessee, fifteen or twenty minutes from us. She'd had a tough, tough life. Pregnant at fourteen, a mama at fifteen, Marcy had quit school to raise her son, Mikel, when she was in the ninth grade, and she never went back. Within a year she was in a shelter for teenage mothers—a government-run place to protect girls like Marcy from the men who said they loved them but had a funny way of showing it. While I was dodging make-believe bullets overhead in boot camp at Parris Island, South Carolina, Marcy was a thousand miles away dodging fists. And she wasn't good at it. Her teeth magically fell out, two or three at a time. They seemed to come loose every time her boyfriend got mad at her.

For the next few years she went through hell. She and her little boy. I came home on leave one weekend and had to spend two hours asking around, just to find out where she was living. She was on the lam but not running from the law. She was running from the guy who was running from the law. Over coffee one morning I saw the new tattoos on her arms and the age in her eyes. She had grown old and wasn't even eighteen yet. I wasn't much help. I think I gave her twenty dollars and a hug and pretended as I drove away that somehow that was gonna fix everything. It didn't.

A couple of years later she came to visit me in California. I had been married only a month or so and was excited that Marcy and her son were coming to stay with us. In our little apartment in Anaheim, it was a fun time to be together again. My sister and I laughed and played in the swimming pool and talked and talked. I thought she was doing well. She said she was, and I believed her. I wouldn't find out 'til much later that she had gotten on that plane in Florida not to come see me but to leave someone. To get over something. To put a hurt behind her that was so deep it would take twenty years to face it and speak even a word of it without losing her breath and almost passing out.

Marcy had had a baby—another baby boy—a day, maybe two, before getting on that plane. And because she and her first son were barely surviving on their own, my sister couldn't bear bringing this one into such an unstable, scary world. So she gave it away. She gave that little bundle of red-haired joy to some wealthy strangers who had things she didn't. Money. A house. A job. Two parents.

She had to get on that airplane. Either that or go running down the street after the fancy car that drove away with her second child. A child that she still has never seen to this day.

Her life would not get much better in the next ten years. It would change but not improve, not much.

She would come live with us again in South Carolina, and again her teeth would be falling out—her face and jaw so swollen you couldn't tell where her chin began and her ear ended. But this time it was not because of fists but because she lacked nutrition. Her teeth turned black and fell out after long, terrible bouts with pain and swelling. But Marcy wouldn't complain. She would just bear that pain and all the rest of it because she had no insurance and no assurance that anything good was on the horizon. The only thing she was sure of was that she loved her son and he loved her.

In time, Marcy met and married a good man. Don Gary. A good,

good man. He drove a trash truck. He still does. He had insurance and provided a trailer for them, then another trailer, and then finally a house. He would be the first bit of stability that she knew—not just in her adult life but in her entire life.

Marcy spent her twenties and thirties waiting tables and bartending, helping Don make ends meet. They had three more beautiful babies together—Magen, Brenda, and Donny. Marcy loved being a mother. Like our mother, it is what she took the most pride in, I think. That and getting a bargain. She loved to take her little ones "garage sale-ing" to see if she could find the best deals. Marcy was a master at it. She often took my kids with them, and when my girls found something they wanted and Aunt Marcy didn't want to pay full price for it, she made sure to say in front of the person hosting the sale, "I'm sorry, honey, but Mama can't afford to buy that for you." And pretty soon, they'd just hand it to my kids and say, "Just take it, baby. It's okay."

Fast-forward a few more years, and Marcy was living on Carter's Creek Pike, not too far from us. I had bought the farmhouse a year or so earlier, and God was working on my character big-time. He was opening my eyes to things that I never saw before. To hurt and pain that was right in front of me that I'd never even noticed. And one day it was Marcy's.

I came up with an idea. I would take a little bit of the money that I had and help Marcy open a restaurant or a secondhand store. Something that could give her some pride. Something that could be her own. I remember when the idea hit me—where I was and what I was doing. It was so random, out of nowhere. But also so real. As if it had already happened or something.

I was going to make Marcy's dreams come true.

And I did, or I was, at least, part of it happening. But not in the way I thought I would be.

There was a little run-down restaurant a mile or so from our farmhouse called Granny's or Pottsville Mercantile or something like that. I had gone in a few times, but it was rough. Really, really rough. I couldn't imagine how it could stay open much longer, so I offered to buy it or lease it. I really had no idea what I was doing. I was thinking that for two thousand dollars, I could do anything! They weren't interested. Not at all.

So I moved on. I called about another place, and the owner told me about a guy in Mount Pleasant who had an empty building across from an old hardware store on the square in that little town. I went down, looked at it, and then leased it. My younger sister, Candy, helped me make it happen. And then one Sunday I invited Marcy and her husband to meet me at a little restaurant on the square in Mount Pleasant called Lumpy's. (I didn't realize it yet, but that restaurant also has a catering hall upstairs called Pearl's Palace, and it would play a big part in my life in the next year or so.) So we all went out to eat. Afterward we walked Marcy down the street, and we looked in the windows of the stores that were closed. She gazed for a long time into one in particular, saying, "Isn't that neat? It looks like there's some old shelves and wooden bins in there." When she turned around, I handed her an envelope. As she opened it up and saw a couple thousand dollars, I said, "It's yours." And she started sobbing. Hysterically. I knew no one had ever done anything like that for her. She couldn't stop crying. I held her as her tears ran down my shirt. It was so, so beautiful.

So she moved her yard-sale stuff in and opened a little store called Aunt Marcy's Uniques and Antiques, and I helped her fix it up. And to be close to her, I rented the hardware store across the street so we could spend time together, have coffee in the mornings, and slow down and enjoy life together. It was heavenly.

Though Marcy wound up selling almost nothing because the town was so run-down and no one was shopping for her brand-new, old "uniques" she had bought at a garage sale the weekend before, something even more beautiful came of it. Joey.

It was because we were there that Lumpy's asked me to start hosting a songwriters' night upstairs, once a week, and it was there that Joey walked in and saw me and changed my path and everyone else's. So though I didn't exactly make Marcy's dreams come true, mine did. And I think it happened because I wasn't worrying about my dreams or my girls or finding someone. I was giving. Instead of taking. For the first time, really.

Within a year Joey and I would be married, and Marcy's little store would shut down. As would my songwriting studio. And we all moved our lives back to Pottsville where our farm was. To the casual observer, it might have looked like we had failed. That I had failed. But I hadn't.

Three years later we were sitting at my kitchen table. Joey, Marcy, and I. And Marcy randomly said, "You know, Jo, you and I should open a little cafe up in that little building down the road that is shut down." And a couple of months later, they did. It became Marcy Jo's Mealhouse. And it changed Marcy's life. And Joey's. And mine. And thousands of others . . . one bite at a time.

Twenty-Eight

MY NAME IS JOEY

She ran up those steps two at a time and landed there, right in front of me. Faded jeans, dusty boots, and a button-up shirt. I had no idea my life was about to change forever.

She had seen me before, I would find out later. At the Bluebird Cafe about two years earlier. I was playing a songwriters' show, and she was in the audience, sitting within a few feet of me. I didn't see her or meet her, at least, not that I can remember, but she remembers it perfectly. She said as she listened to me sing the songs I had written and tell my stories, she had this feeling come over her that I was the one. That we were going to spend the rest of our lives together. She told me that too. It wouldn't be for another two years, but that was one of the first things she told me when we finally got the chance to meet and talk.

But that night at the Bluebird, she didn't say anything. Something inside her just knew. The way the Canadian geese that fly over our farmhouse know when it's time to make their way south or head north for home at winter's end. No one can explain how they know . . . they just know.

As that night at the Bluebird wore on, I introduced my daughters, Heidi and Hopie, to the audience. Joey said she thought to herself, *Aw, he's married. What a shame. All the good ones are already taken.* Then she went on with her life, working at a horse vet clinic and trying to find her way in music.

That was in 2000, and she had moved to Nashville two years earlier, from her hometown of Alexandria, Indiana. Known as the hometown of gospel legend Bill Gaither, it was an hour northeast of Indianapolis and a million miles from Music City, where Joey had dreamed of moving since she was a little girl. Dolly Parton was her hero. She had learned "Coat of Many Colors" when she was three or four years old. Before she could read, she had taken a cassette tape upstairs in the farmhouse where she grew up and did not come back down until she knew the whole song by heart.

Alexandria (locals call it Alex . . . spoken like "Elek") was a wonderful little community, and the seventies and eighties were a wonderful time to grow up there. Her father, Jack Martin, played guitar and worked for General Motors, and her mother, June, was a stay-at-home mother who had the voice of a honky-tonk angel. They had met in high school and had played in a band together. Both having dreams of doing something more with their music, before diapers and paychecks became the goal and five little mouths the priority. Joey had two older sisters, Jody and Julie; a younger brother, Justin; and a baby sister, Jessie. Joey spent her days playing in the corncrib and barns and riding her bike to neighbors' houses until she was old enough to buy her first horse. From then on she rode Velvet everywhere she went. She said, for three or four years in a row, she went as the Headless Horseman for Halloween and trick-or-treated from a saddle.

Those were great memories for her. As were her times of singing with her parents. They played local fairs and VFWs, and any other place that would let her sing, while her daddy played his twelve-string Guild guitar. Music was always her gift. Her voice was special, everyone said back then. They say the same thing now, nearly a lifetime later.

When Joey graduated high school in 1994, she was still singing and set her sights on Nashville. She knew that was where she wanted and needed to be, but she didn't know how she was going to get there. She worked for a horse vet for the next two years, then transferred to a vet in Tennessee. That was how she got here. Joey was always practical. Even her dreaming was practical.

Once in Nashville, she took a unique approach to becoming famous. She worked with horses. That was her plan. She would do what she knew how to do and hope that it would lead somewhere. And it did. Through the horse world, she would meet Kix Brooks's wife and then Kix (of Brooks & Dunn). And LeAnn Rimes's father, Wilbur. They all saw something in her—first in her character and then her talent—and wanted to help. In time, she found herself with a record deal on Sony Records and with Paul Worley, of Dixie Chicks fame, producing an album with her. That's where I showed up, again.

—⁘—

Joey was still working for a horse vet clinic in Thompson's Station, south of Nashville, and one day Bob McCullough, one of the doctors at the clinic, told her he was going out to see his neighbor Tim Johnson. Tim was a songwriter performing that night, along with another guy named Rory Lee. Joey said she got a big smile on her face when she heard my name and told Dr. Bob about the time she'd seen me play at the Bluebird a few years earlier. She told him that if I hadn't been married with kids, she would've thought we were meant to be together. Then Bob explained to her that I wasn't married and that I'd been a single father for the last twelve years.

Joey said she hightailed it home and got ready, then made a beeline to Mount Pleasant to see if the feelings she had before were still there.

I was already at Pearl's Palace, getting the tables and sound ready for the night's show when Joey came walking in. It was a weekly songwriter show that I was putting together in this new venue, and I wanted everything to be just right. I was walking toward the stairs when I saw these long legs come bounding up the steps and this gorgeous raven-haired woman land right in front of me.

The evening is looking up, I thought. "Hello," I said. She sorta smiled and said hi back.

"I'm Rory," I told her.

"Joey," she said. "My name's Joey."

And my world changed forever.

I didn't know it at the time. You never know these things when they're happening. They seem like normal, everyday occurrences—like nothing special is happening, but it is. The world is shifting and up is about to be down and right is about to be left, and the life you knew before isn't ever going to be the same.

I guess we stood there and chatted for a minute. Me asking her what had brought her there and her saying she was meeting friends to watch the show. I was friendly to her, but she was very standoffish to me. I remember seeing her from my stool on the stage. I can still picture the table where she was sitting with her friends. I wondered how such a beautiful girl had walked into a place like this. So far from Nashville, where all the beautiful women seem to congregate.

But then the next week she showed up again. And she was again sitting at a table watching me and three other songwriters perform. I thought, *That's strange.* Because this time the only songwriter onstage she knew was me. Was she coming back just to see me?

After the show a bunch of us walked down the block to my office. I had turned the old hardware store on the square in Mount Pleasant into a songwriting studio about six months earlier. Inside, I had a couple of couches, a piano, and an old soda machine where I kept small Coke bottles. Somehow Joey followed our group there and sat with us. I tried to talk with her, but she really didn't say much. She was still standoffish. I remember thinking it was clear that she wasn't interested in me. I had learned by then that she had a record deal and was looking for songs to record, so I asked her if I could play a few of my songs for her. If nothing else, maybe she would record one. She wrote something on a piece of paper and handed it to me. "You can mail them to my P.O. box," she said as she walked out. I knew then for sure where I stood with her. Nowhere.

A week or so went by, and I realized that along with her address, she had also written a phone number on the piece of paper. So I called it and got a machine. I left a message. A few days went by, and I didn't get a call back. God had been working on me, and I could read the signs. They all said, "This girl doesn't like you." But later that week, something made me call her one last time. I left her a voice mail that said I was calling her one last time and I added, "If you want to call me back, here is my home number." I figured that was the end of that. But, around nine that evening, the phone rang.

I had just put the girls to bed and was sitting on the couch in the living room when she called. I recognized the number on the caller ID, so I picked up the phone and casually said, "Hello?"

The voice on the other end said, "This is Joey. I want to tell you why I've been cold and distant to you." Then as I listened, with my jaw hanging open, she told me about seeing me at the Bluebird a couple years before and feeling inside that we were going to spend the rest of our lives together and how she saw my kids and thought I was married. She told me about the doctor telling her I wasn't married and that she'd come to the show in Mount Pleasant that first night to see if the feelings she originally had for me were still there. "They were," she said. So she came back the next week too. She told me how nervous she had been to talk to me because it was as if God was saying, "Him . . . that is who you're going to marry."

I thought, *This must be a hoax. Maybe my friend Tim Johnson has gone to elaborate lengths to pull one over on his buddy.* I'd never heard of such a thing—especially coming from such a beautiful girl. I thought, *If this is real, I might have just won the lottery!*

But then she told me she was dating a wonderful guy, up in Indiana, and that they'd been together for a year and a half and she was probably going to marry him. But she wanted to tell me that if things were different, if the timing were better, maybe she and I would be together.

I was dumbfounded. It was too much to believe, but I played along.

"So I *was* your destiny, but now somebody else is?" She said yes, that was how it seemed. I thought, *This is the craziest thing I've ever heard.* But I also thought it was pretty awesome in a weird sort of way. Then I half-jokingly asked her, "Can we meet for coffee sometime . . . so I can see who it is that I missed out on marrying?"

Surprisingly, she said yes, and we made a date to meet for coffee the next Saturday morning at the truck stop by my exit.

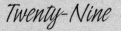

Twenty-Nine

A GIRL, A DOG, AND A TRUCK

Something inside told me, *This is it. This is her. This is what God has been preparing you for.*

When I walked into Stan's Truck Stop, Joey was already there. Stan's is like a Cracker Barrel—before there were Cracker Barrels all over the South—filled with aisles of knickknacks in the main room and a restaurant in the back. She was standing in an aisle, looking at something or other, when I said hello. She turned around and said hello back. I just stood there, staring at her. Looking her up and down. I'm sure she thought I was a weirdo. But this girl didn't look like anything I'd ever seen before. Her long dark hair fell down on her faded Carhartt barn coat, with sleeves frayed from hundreds of hours of working in the cold and stains on the sleeves from "horse placenta," as she would tell me a little while later, during our conversation over coffee.

We sat at a table near the window and talked a long, long time. Her telling me about her life and me telling her about mine. Something in her eyes made me feel like I could be honest. Like I could tell her the truth about who I was and who I was trying to be. About my girls and about growing up the way I did. I'm pretty sure, at some point, I cried, and she reached out her hand, her fingers wrapped around mine. I looked up to find the softest, kindest brown eyes I'd ever seen, looking not just into my eyes but into my soul. And it was over.

I felt a voice inside of me saying, *This is the one I have chosen for you,* but I couldn't believe it. It was too real, too good. Too much like magic. I'd written plenty of songs about magic and about people falling in love with just a look or a touch, but that stuff wasn't real. It was just make-believe. It was the stuff in movies. A *Sleepless in Seattle* story, made up by brilliant writers who know how to manipulate heartstrings with the right words and the right music playing at the right time. But there was no music—only the sounds of pans clanging in the kitchen and men with Farm Co-op caps in booths talking about rain coming in and the timing of the hay that needed cutting.

But I didn't hear any of it. Or see it. All I could see was Joey, and all I could feel was that moment.

Joey had brought some homemade bread with her to the restaurant. She had baked it the night before. As she unwrapped it and cut me a slice, she told me about her life and her dreams. How her mom had helped her load all her stuff into a cattle trailer and she'd made the trip to Nashville without really knowing anyone. How she had dated a cowboy for a few years and it hadn't worked out. About her sisters and how they were having babies and she didn't have that desire inside of her. That maybe music was her baby. How she loved to sing in the choir at the church she attended. And how she cried at baptisms.

Then she told me about her record deal, how they were almost done with the album and how excited she was about it. How she worked at a vet clinic and loved making the rounds to different farms with the doctors. She only took time off to sing in the studio and then came right back to work.

An hour turned into three, and soon the banana nut bread she'd made was all gone. I walked her to her car—a black Dodge truck that was parked around back. Her dog, Rufus, was in the bed, sleeping in the shade she had parked under. Joey introduced me, and I watched her rub his ears and him melt into her touch. It was easy to see this was her best friend. And she was his. I gave her a hug good-bye, and she drove off.

As I made my way back under the interstate toward my farmhouse, I called my sister Candy on my cell phone. "I just had coffee with someone,"

I told her. "You don't know her, and neither do I, really. She's in the music business, and I don't want to be with someone in the industry. I have kids, and she doesn't want children. And she's in a serious relationship with a doctor in Indiana." Candy listened on. "Anyway . . . we're headed in opposite directions, but I have this weird feeling that I was just looking into the eyes of my destiny. I felt I needed to call and tell someone."

My sister had never heard me talk that way about someone and knew it was a big deal for me to say that. I didn't know what had just happened, but I knew enough to know that it felt different from anything else I'd ever experienced. I told her I wanted to tell her about it so we could pay attention and see if anything came of it.

Nothing probably would. But then again, you never know.

Thirty

NOTHING TO REMEMBER

I'm thankful for the day we met
that evening in September
'cause I'd rather have something to forget
than nothing to remember.

Our truck-stop date was in the fall of 2001. Weeks went by, and Joey and I would talk on the phone now and then. Mostly, I would call and check in with her to see how she was doing. More than once she told me that she would be going back to Indiana that coming weekend to see the guy she was dating, and she thought that maybe he was going to propose to her or, at least, ask her dad for permission to marry her. I would sorta laugh and say once again, "So let me get this right. . . . I *was* your destiny, but now this guy is? And you're gonna marry him?" She would say yes, very matter-of-factly. Then I would talk with her the next week and find out that he had been busy in his work and hadn't gotten around to talking to her dad or asking her. I found that very interesting.

At the time, I was writing songs for a publishing company on Music Row, so I invited Joey to come with me and my girls to a CMA Viewing Party that was going to be happening in a few days. They had a big catered event every year in a large tent behind their building to watch the Country Music Awards. She agreed to go with us. That was our first date. Sort of.

I was actually dating another girl at the time. She was young and fun, and the kids loved her, and, of course, Joey was dating the doctor in Indianapolis. So we couldn't technically go on a date. But we spent the evening together listening to and watching the music we both loved so much on a big screen, and I got to see Joey around my girls and just be with her. It was easy to see that she was special.

A few days later we got together to write a song. I proposed that we write about a couple who wasn't able to be together long-term but was thankful for the little bit of time they had with each other. She thought that idea maybe hit a little too close to home. I told her that was the point . . . let's write what we couldn't say. The result was the first song we ever wrote together called "Nothing to Remember."

Like Joey, the song was special, and I knew it. It's still special. I have the original recording we did of it. She and I sat on the carpet in her little apartment in Franklin, Tennessee. Me on guitar, Joey singing. By the time we did the full demo, we had changed the words of the first verse. She was afraid that someone might see through the lyrics and realize that this song was more than just a made-up story. That there was some truth in it. The original lyrics had talked about how she had come to a place with another guy and heard me sing and that's how we met . . . but we made it that she randomly ran into me in a store. It was safer that way.

The afternoon that I was in the recording studio mixing the song, Joey's boyfriend happened to be in town visiting her. She brought him to the studio to hear the mix. It's the only time I ever met him. He was wonderful. I could see why she liked him. It was a little surreal, listening back to the song with her and him sitting on the couch beside me . . . listening to the new lyrics we'd written to hide the words and emotion we both felt. It felt wrong but not really. Joey would never do anything that wasn't honoring to him or to God. Or even to me. It was who she was. I wasn't quite there yet, but I was getting closer.

Joey was the person who would help me fully realize the potential of my character and walk with God. I didn't know it yet, but in a few months' time, she would be the rock by my side that would change everything.

Especially me.

Thirty-One

SIGN LANGUAGE

I asked for God to give me a sign. . . . He gave me a building-sized billboard.

Joey and I kept in touch and would talk to and see each other now and then, but it was clear that she was headed in one direction and I was headed in the other. And just as she had told me: if the timing had been different, things might've worked out for us.

I was okay with that. I really was. I didn't expect anything, especially anything good. It was too good to be true, and that made it easy for me to dismiss. If something like this happened (or almost happened) in years past, I would've been stressing over it. Working every angle to try to make it happen. But that's not where I was. God had me somewhere different. I had been putting my future in His hands and was feeling good about leaving it there. I have a feeling that's part of why it came to be in the end . . . because I was okay with it, even if it didn't.

Maybe that's how God's logic works. You have to be okay with not having something to be given it. I think about that often: God's logic. Things like . . . he who is least is greatest. Whoever is last is first. Give it away if you want to keep it. Die to really live. It doesn't really make sense on paper, but it works. And that's all that matters.

—m—

I got a call from Joey on Valentine's Day. It was late morning, and she said that she had broken up with the doctor. That he was supposed to come down that weekend but was too busy with work. She had given him three chances, and this had been his third and final chance. They were over. She said if I wanted to spend time with her, she was available and would like that. The vet clinic she worked for was having a little Valentine's get-together that evening, and she wanted to know if I'd like to come with her. As her date.

I didn't really have to think about it. I knew the answer.

I hung up the phone and called the girl I was dating and told her it was over. We just didn't work out. I know that probably hurt her, but we had been dating only a short while. God had just moved a mountain, right in front of me. And I was going to see what was on the other side.

I spent the evening with Joey, her coworkers, and the doctors she worked for. They were all wonderful. I could see that they loved her. Joey was a hard worker and incredibly devoted to her job. To anything she committed to. But I also learned that when she turned a corner and was finished with something, such as her ex-boyfriend, she never looked back. I filed that away. *This is a woman who means business. She won't break up with me and later want to get back together, letting drama run her life and mine for months on end as it had in the last couple of relationships I'd had.* For Joey, commitment was a one-time thing. I could tell with her, things were gonna be different.

The truth is, Joey wasn't what I was looking for. I'm ashamed to say that, but it's true. I had always dated voluptuous women, and Joey was tall and thin. With the girls I dated I had always felt a physical chemistry first (part of the reason why I made bad choices), and then I looked to see how compatible we were afterward. With Joey, I wasn't really feeling the chemistry. It was more about the strange magic and the circumstances surrounding her that enamored me. And I knew that if this were to turn into a forever thing, forever is a long time to go without chemistry and deep attraction for someone.

I asked my sister Candy about it and told her my dilemma. She had been following our progress since the first time I'd called her after our truck-stop meeting, and she was excited to see this next step that Joey and I were taking.

She asked me, "What if what you really need is something that you don't know you need?" She continued, "What if what's on the other side of this is the greatest love and chemistry you've ever felt . . . even though you might not feel it right now?"

I responded, "But what if it isn't?" Something inside of me was telling me that Joey was the one, but I still wasn't completely sure. I needed a sign. I wanted one. So I prayed that God would send me a sign. That He would show me, clearly, that she was the one for me.

I was playing another show at the Bluebird Cafe, and Joey was there with me and Candy. Joey's mother was in town visiting her and was there also. Near the end of the show, Joey got up and sang "Nothing to Remember" with me. Afterward, she and her mom invited us to come to Joey's apartment for coffee and some dessert. As we sat in her apartment, we started talking about our childhoods, about how we'd gotten interested in music. Joey said that her mom and dad sang while she was growing up and that her dad played guitar. I said, "My dad played guitar when I was growing up."

She said they used to sing songs that she didn't know . . . songs from long ago that her parents grew up on. I said, "My dad sang songs that I never heard on the radio, songs from long ago too." Then I asked Joey, "Like, what kinda songs?" And she picked up the guitar sitting by her chair and played the chorus of "Have I Told You Lately That I Love You."

My sister started crying. She got up out of the rocking chair where she was sitting and ran to the bathroom. Chills were rolling down my back. Joey stopped singing and said, "What's wrong?" She had no idea what she had just done. But Candy knew, and so did I.

My father only knew about ten songs that he played and sang on guitar. He probably knew more, but there were only about ten that he sang most of our childhood. The one we heard the most was Jim Reeves's "Have I Told You Lately That I Love You." Recorded originally in the

1950s, Dad sang it our whole lives. And when my father died in 1988, it was the only song played at his funeral. That's why Candy was crying.

I never questioned if Joey was the one for me again. Ever. I just trusted that God had brought her into my life for a reason, and He would show me how and why and everything else I needed to know when the time came.

Within a few weeks Joey and I were talking about marriage. I don't know why; we just did. We barely knew each other, but we knew we were made for each other and that was enough. Joey wanted to be married. She always had. I would learn that marriage was part of what would make her world complete. And as well as her music or life was going, she wouldn't be fulfilled until she was a wife with a husband to love and take care of.

I knew this relationship was different, and to protect it, I wanted to do things differently. Be different. Joey did too. I had a past. A long list of sins and habits that still wanted to be part of my life. Joey had a very short list. She wasn't perfect. She'd made some mistakes. Had a few regrets, but nothing compared to mine.

We committed to doing the right thing. To waiting until we were married before we would consummate our relationship. By then, I was almost thirty-seven, and Joey was twenty-six. I had lived a lot of life, and that physical intimacy had been a big part of relationships, and my life, for a long time. I even had two kids. To try to be with someone without "being with" someone wasn't gonna be easy. But I also knew that's how God said it was supposed to be. And it was something I'd never tried before.

Maybe it would make a difference. If we honored Him, maybe He would honor our relationship.

Thirty-Two

THE RIGHT LEFT HAND

I wrote this song about my wife—but I sang it for a few girlfriends before I met her." That's how I would always start out singing "Teaching Me How to Love You"—one of the songs that Joey and I would sing for years together onstage each night. And it was true. There were things that I went through with other people . . . hard things . . . that were all for Joey. They were opportunities for me to learn something, so I could be ready when she came along. I didn't understand it then, but in time I would.

—⁓—

The first time I brought Joey to our farmhouse, the one that would soon be home to her for the rest of her life, the place was still rough, but she loved it. I had done a good bit of work on it by then to try to make it more livable, and it was. But it was far from nice. Joey told me it was perfect, the kind of house where she could make a life and be happy.

I wouldn't understand why until a month or so later when I made the trip to see the house where she grew up and realized who she was, where she came from, and what she was about. Joey wasn't a cul-de-sac-in-a-suburb-outside-the-city kinda girl. Where the houses all look alike and are right next to each other. She would need space to grow a large garden, hardwood floors that have been lived on, and a porch to see the stars from at night. Like me, she liked character. Old things with charm and potential appealed to her more than new, nice things.

For the next fourteen years Joey and I could be driving down the road and see a run-down house covered in weeds, with the porch falling off and the tin-roof caved in. Deserted, looking as though it hadn't been lived in for twenty years, and we'd look at each other and say, "Wow, did you see that?" It wasn't unusual for us to pull over and walk around, just imagining how life must have been for the families who grew up there and wonder, "How could anyone let this place get so run-down?"

That's who Joey was, and I had become very similar.

We were sitting on the bed next to each other one evening, talking about the future, and I asked her what kind of engagement ring she wanted. She thought about it, then said, "Something old, I think. Maybe something antique that has some personality and history to it." *That's strange*, I thought. Then I remembered something but thought, *No, I shouldn't mention it.* But Joey kept talking about how she liked silver and platinum and diamonds that have unique cuts to them. So I got up from the bed and walked across the room to the dresser.

From the back of my sock drawer, I pulled out a little leather box and nervously carried it over and sat beside her on the bed. "You mean, like this one?" I opened the box, and inside was exactly what she had described. An antique engagement ring from the 1920s made of platinum, with little blue sapphires on the sides and an oval-shaped diamond sparkling on the top. Joey's eyes lit up.

"It's not what you think," I said. "I bought it for another girl a couple of years ago. I gave it to her. A few times. I was trying to make something terrible work. It ended up being thrown across the floor of an Alan Jackson concert. And I just never figured out what to do with it. I need to take it somewhere and sell it."

Joey slowly slid it on her finger . . . and it fit. Perfectly. "Don't get rid of it," she said. "I'll wear it if you ever decide that you want to ask me."

What? I thought. *What is she talking about? She should be mad at me right now. Pissed that I still even have such a thing or that I would show it to her.* Instead, Joey treated me as though I had done something good by buying that ring and hanging on to it . . . as if I had just given it to the wrong person. She made me feel like all the ring needed was time . . . to find the right left hand.

God, I loved her.

Thirty-Three

A CLEAN SLATE

There comes a time when you have to put your past . . . well, in your past.

None of it mattered to Joey. She listened as I told her what I'd been through. The terrible things I'd done and the person I'd been. How I had cheated on girls and been cheated on and how I'd made a wreck of my life and others'. She listened, but she didn't judge. The things I said and confessed hurt her. But not in the way you'd think. They hurt her . . . for me. The tears would roll down her cheeks, and she would tell me how sorry she was that I had to go through all that. That I had to experience those things at all. She never made me feel bad for them. Or for one moment believed that the man I was before was the man that I would be in the future. She just let it all go.

How do you do that? I had been in plenty of relationships before Joey, and in most of them, we had fought about our pasts. We'd made each other burn photos of past girlfriends or boyfriends and made each other confess things we had done, only to use those confessions against each other like weapons. To destroy the other person when they disappointed us, or when we were feeling jealous or guilty or when we just felt bad about ourselves. Joey wasn't like that. She just let my past stay in the past . . . and wiped the slate clean.

"Aren't you afraid that I might cheat on you?" I said one day when I worked up the nerve to ask.

"No," she said. "You chose to be with me. Why would I think you would want to be with someone else?" For her, it was that simple. Everything was.

Life is black-and-white for Joey. It's one of her gifts. She doesn't torture herself with the thousand shades of gray that my mind can go to. She only knows good and bad. Right and wrong. What a gift God has given her. And me, by being beside her.

It took me a few years to learn to trust her the way she trusted me. It was tough for her to live with me for the first year or so, because I was always afraid she might find someone she loved more than me. That she was attracted to more. But, in time, I learned that all the energy I spent in fear and jealousy was just wasted life. I would come to realize that if Joey said she was going to be somewhere or do something, that's what she would do. She didn't lie. Not ever. *Who doesn't lie from time to time?* I thought. *Or at least stretch the truth?* Well . . . her. That's who. And she would teach me that the things that had drug me down didn't need to anymore. "If you just tell the truth," she would say, "you don't ever have to remember anything." What a huge difference that little bit of information has made in my life. In fact, all the small, big things she taught me over the years have made all the difference in my life.

In time, jealousy disappeared from my mind and heart. I don't know how or when. I just woke up one day, and it was gone. It's still gone. It's not in me anymore to be jealous. Joey impacted my character to the core and changed how I'm wired. I'm not saying that I couldn't screw up and rewire myself in the future and relearn those old habits, but at least I know it's possible to change . . . to *really* change. I never knew that before. I figured that what I was, was what I always would be. What I struggled with, I would always struggle with. But it doesn't have to be that way.

Love, real love, is stronger than all of that.

Thirty-Four

CROSSING OUR HEARTS

Joey's home became my home, and my home became hers.

In mid-April, two months after we started dating, Joey and my girls and I took a trip together to Joey's hometown in Indiana to spend some time with her mom, dad, and three sisters—Jody, Julie, and Jessie—and to see where Joey had grown up.

It was dark by the time we exited I-69 and pulled into the driveway. Joey's mother, June, met us at the door of the late-1800s farmhouse they lived in—the one where Joey was born and had grown up. To say that it was warm and charming and perfect is an understatement. It is a good-sized white-frame house, like ours, with a tin roof and a wood-burning stove in the living room, surrounded by barns and large shade trees outside. Near the biggest barn, the Green Goose—a broken-down 1965 Chevy truck that Joey and all the kids first learned how to drive in—was turning to rust.

We stepped from a small porch almost immediately into the kitchen. Farm-life paintings and a feed sack lined the walls, and knickknacks filled the shelves above the sink—but not the kind of knickknacks you see in a lot of people's houses, where they're just there to make a place look homey. Everything here had a history, its place in the story of the Martins' lives.

Joey walked us through the house, and I dropped my bag in the upstairs bedroom that used to be hers. Sparsely decorated with beautiful wallpaper and a small lamp on the bedside table. Her mother came and sat in a rocking chair beside Joey and me. "What are you two up to?" she asked. And we told her.

We explained that we had been dating for two months and wanted to get married. That I was going to ask Joey's daddy for permission to take her hand. I think that came as quite a shock to Joey's mama. She knew that her third daughter had never wanted children, and I had two. Not just two kids . . . two teenage daughters. Something that could make this quick romance story even harder for June and everyone else to believe was a good idea. But she listened as we told her how we had a feeling that God was leading us down this path and that we wanted to honor Him in all our choices. And to honor her and her ex-husband, Jack.

Joey's parents had divorced more than a half-dozen years before, after their only son's death had taken its toll on their family. Justin, a year younger than Joey, was seventeen at the time and was on his way to the county fair that July evening in '94, when the car accident happened a half mile from their farmhouse. A car had been parked on the side of the road with no lights on, and Justin's jeep plowed into the back of it, throwing him from the vehicle, his girlfriend buckled in the passenger seat . . . and Justin without his seat belt.

Joey and her mama got a call from a neighbor and were two of the first people to arrive at the scene, long before the paramedics. There in that ditch, Joey held her brother's hand as his lungs struggled to find air, and their mother prayed for God to intervene and save her only son.

God was busy that night, I guess, or at least that's how Joey's daddy looked at it. A week later the doctors told them there was nothing else they could do, and they turned off the machines that had kept him alive. Jack had prayed like he'd never prayed before, and still Justin died.

Faith was replaced by anger and resentment, and it would be years and years before Jack would reevaluate his faith in God and whether God could actually love us and let our children pass away, right before our eyes. Joey would lead him to that place . . . to the only real peace he'd had in his heart in twenty years. But it cost him, not only those years of his life but hers too.

Justin's pictures lined the shelves in the living room, and photo albums were stacked end to end in the hallway. A large white metal cross was installed in the ditch just down the lane where they had prayed over him, to remind them and everyone who drove by that their boy had lived and died on this stretch of Indiana road.

Joey's parents never got over their loss and divorced a year or so later. Their relationship had been strained already. June wanted a life of simple living on the small farm they were making payments on, but Jack wanted more. Much more. He would find it in a new wife and a new life eight miles away in town. And June would have the life she loved forever, but without someone to share it with. A compromise, I think, where everyone lost. Especially their kids.

When Joey and I finished talking, June hugged her daughter, me, and the girls and told them that she would support us and would take Joey shopping for a dress when the time was right—that is, after I asked Jack. And Joey.

The next evening all of Joey's family showed up at the house, and June cooked a huge meal. Joey's Aunt Wanda and Uncle Shirl were there and Joey's three sisters and their husbands, boyfriend, and kids. I loved them all. It was like being dropped into a life that I'd always dreamed of but had never known. After dinner Joey's daddy got out his twelve-string guitar and played while she sang "Have I Told You Lately That I Love You" and "Coat of Many Colors." She also sang "In the Garden" with her mother. It was magical. To me it was.

Later that evening, long after everyone had gone home after the dinner, we called Joey's daddy and asked him to put on a pot of coffee. Then Joey and I drove to his house and sat with him at his new place, and I asked him for permission to marry his daughter. Jack was caught off guard, to say the least, and explained that she had been dating a different guy just a couple of months before. He had thought that guy was going to be the one popping the question about popping the question. He worried that we were rushing things. We agreed that we were. But Joey also said, "When you know, Dad, you know." I think he tried to talk us out of it, but he probably realized that our minds were already made up, and he gave me his approval.

When we got back to her mama's house, as Joey stepped out of the truck, I took her hand and asked her to take a walk with me. By now, it was about 2 a.m. In the dark, we walked down the lane she grew up on. The road where she had ridden her bike a thousand times and gone trick-or-treating, house to house, on her horse, Velvet. We walked and walked and dreamed and talked. The moon was bright, and it lit up the sky and farmland like it was daytime. When we got to the other side of the four-way stop, I got down on my knee.

"Joey Marie Martin, will you marry me?" I asked. Tears rolled down her cheeks. I knew what this moment meant to her, how long she had been waiting for it. Not from me but from God. Of course, she had known I was going to ask her sometime. Today, or tomorrow or the next week, but she didn't know it would be right then. Right there. A few feet from us was the white metal cross marking the place where her heart and her family had been shattered into pieces years before. I wanted to change that for her. To let that be the place where a beautiful new life began and not just where one ended.

We were both still crying when I heard her sweet voice say, "I will."

Thirty-Five

ALTER CALL

We were married two months later, on June 15, 2002. It was her brother Justin's birthday. He would have been twenty-five.

It was also the fifth wedding anniversary for my cousin and best man, Aaron, and his wife, Jill. Their life and love story had paralleled ours for many years, and having our wedding on their anniversary was just one more God-wink in a long list of them.

I wish I could tell you that I paid for our wedding, but I didn't. Joey did. She had received a fifteen-thousand-dollar bonus for signing her record deal a few months earlier, and she took that money and used it to pay most of the costs for the wedding and the reception. I had made a good bit of money in the past couple of years on royalties from songs I'd written but, unfortunately, hadn't been very responsible with it. Joey just stepped up and took care of it all. In the coming months we would have many conversations about money, and she would put her foot down and set me on a better path toward financial responsibility—but for now, she didn't say a word. She just wrote the checks from her account and made our beautiful wedding happen.

The ceremony was at a little church in Mount Pleasant, the same small town where Joey and I had met and where I'd had my songwriting studio at the time. Her mother was her maid of honor, and her sisters and Heidi and Hopie were her bridesmaids. Rufus, Joey's trusty hound, was the ring bearer. We had about three hundred people in attendance, and afterward we held the reception a block away at Pearl's Palace—the same place where Joey had bounded up the steps and landed in front of me the night I met her at my songwriters' show.

It was a magical day. Joey looked like an angel in her wedding gown, and though I felt a little foolish in the tux I was wearing (instead of my usual overalls), I mostly felt honored to be standing beside her. To be taking her hand and walking her down the aisle. Black-and-white and color pictures from that afternoon and evening fill the pages of a beautiful handmade album at home now, but the memories I have will last a lifetime.

Joey's mama and daddy played and sang "Have I Told You Lately That I Love You," and we lit a candle for Justin. When the "I Dos" had been said, we descended the steps of the church, with rice raining down, and climbed into my old '56 Chevy to make our getaway, with fifteen Dr. Pepper cans tied to the back bumper—a reference to how much I loved Forrest Gump, the fictional character of a man I aspired to be more like.

Joey and I were ready to start our new lives together. To see what God had in store for us. We knew He had brought us together, and we had stepped out in faith and trusted Him. We had no idea of the choppy waters ahead of us, before the wind would finally die down and smooth sailing would carry us halfway around the world on a song and then back again.

Thirty-Six

SEXUAL HEALING

O ur first time was on our wedding night.

It's true. That might not seem like a big deal to most people, but it is. Especially since I was thirty-seven years old, had two teenage children, and had done more than my fair share of living by then. *Purity* wasn't a word, or virtue, that I had even considered making a real part of my life, but it was what Joey and I now wanted most of all. To start out our marriage, and our lives together, right.

I had been told by my Christian friends for years and years about how God designed love to be pure and how saving yourself for marriage was the right thing. But I always thought, *Surely God and my married Bible-thumping buddies don't understand how hard it is these days.* How much sense it makes to "take 'er for a few test spins" before buying the car. I'd done a lot of test-driving in my past, and the outcome was always the same. I got bored with the car long before I ever got to the point of signing papers to own it. That made it easy and convenient to move on, but it didn't make for something long lasting. For the thing that I wanted more than anything. Forever.

For a while I thought all I really needed was a virtuous woman. Maybe that would make the difference. One who had the character and strength that I didn't so she could help me make the right decisions and do the right things. But that didn't work. Instead of the girl helping me, I just corrupted her. I hated the truth of it, but the problem was inside of me. So, the solution had to lie there also.

My whole life, I had always wanted to be with a great woman. Someone I was in awe of. A woman with integrity that I had complete respect for. But as it turns out, in order for me to be with a great woman, I was gonna have to learn to be a great man first. A man of honor and character. Of God. Someone who put others' needs first, before his own. If I was honest with myself, that seemed too hard to achieve. Impossible, actually. So I gave up. And gave in. And I gave it to God.

Sexual sin, selfishness, lust, greed . . . they're all part of the same thing. The desire to make it be about what we desire, instead of what He wants for us. Once I started letting Him have it and really trusting Him, the hard decisions became a little easier to make. And good and honorable are things I just became, not because I set out to become them but because I set out to become His. By following and trusting Him, He molded and changed me into something worthy of His love. And, in turn, worthy of the love of a woman like Joey too.

Saving ourselves for our wedding night wasn't easy for me or for Joey. But it wasn't difficult either, in a different way. Joey and I wanted God's blessing on our marriage, more than we wanted what we wanted. We did our best to keep ourselves out of situations that would get us in trouble, and, of course, we got married four months after we started dating. That helped too.

As we lit candles late that special evening following our wedding, we took each other's hands and kissed . . . we stopped and knelt down beside the big king-size bed I'd just bought for us. Unspoiled and clean, like our commitment to each other. The bed where we would lie together for the next fourteen years and dream of making music and a life together and, in time, holding a baby in our arms. And we got down on our knees and prayed.

We prayed that God would bless this union. And bless this house and the children in it. That He would put and keep His hand upon us and guide us where He wanted us to go.

'Til death do us part.

Thirty-Seven

HONEYMOONERS

T he honeymoon was hell.

Not completely, but it definitely wasn't heaven for us. Not even close.

A friend of mine had offered to let us use his cabin in the Bitterroot Mountains outside of Darby, Montana, for a week. So we arranged for Heidi and Hopie to be at their favorite summer camp while we were away. Joey and I packed a few things, dropped off the kids at Camp Marymount, and hopped a plane, headed west for ten days of newly married bliss together in paradise.

What awaited us in Montana was reality. The truth of where we were and the issues we hadn't faced yet. There were two large problems that we hadn't dealt with.

One, Joey was a singer with a career that was about to take off—at least, it looked like it would. There was a good chance she would be going out on the road soon, for days, weeks, and months at a time. And I didn't want to be left at home, in the same situation I'd been in for years— raising kids by myself without someone to share life with. And I didn't want to be with someone in the music business. I'd already done that. More than once. And it hadn't ended well. It always turned into lies, then cheating, then my heart being broken in a gazillion pieces. I didn't want that to happen.

Two, Joey didn't want children. And I had two. Two teenage girls who desperately needed a woman in their lives. A mother. But Joey didn't want to be a mother; she just wanted to be my wife. It was nothing at all against Heidi or Hopie. It wasn't them. It was her. When God had passed out the gene to girls that made them want to make, have, change, and raise babies, Joey was in the line getting the "sing like Dolly Parton" gene. It wasn't in her, and no amount of talking or arguing or pleading would put it there. For the next ten years, I couldn't put a baby in her arms. She just didn't have a maternal instinct in the least.

Something inside me told me that this was a big issue for her, and that one day it would come back around on her, and she would have to deal with it—but it definitely wasn't going to happen on our honeymoon or anytime soon. Just like I wasn't ready to deal with my fear of Joey being away from me on the road, doing God knows what with a bunch of musicians that I didn't trust.

And so our honeymoon was tough. We had some good moments. Some nice dinners and a wonderful hike up a mountainside. But mostly it was hard. Me plowing head-on into these issues and her avoiding them. Me trying to get her to come my way and understand my needs . . . while having no interest in understanding hers.

We each had our own agenda, and we carried them into our marriage. My friend and pastor, Mike Rosser, had met with Joey and me at a Cracker Barrel a few weeks before we got married to talk with us about the upcoming ceremony he would perform and to make sure we understood the commitment we were making. He asked a few questions and listened to us argue for a while, then said, "Oh, no, you two can't get married! This is a disaster. You have too many big issues to work out." He pleaded with us to put it off for a while, to take our time and work through the potential problems before we made a big mistake by getting married. We told him that we had faith and felt strongly about getting married now, and somehow these things would work themselves out.

But down deep inside, I don't think Joey or I thought they would. How could they? They were too big. My insecurities and her headstrong ways. So we cried a lot of tears in Montana, and then we came home and cried a bunch more.

Joey thought that I understood that this was who she was and how it was going to be. I didn't. I wanted her to throw it all away and quit singing.

I thought Joey understood my situation—that the kids needed a mom and I needed a wife who was going to be home with us. She didn't. She thought that since I had been a single father for so long already, I would be fine with her being gone and we could just have a long-distance marriage if that's what it took.

I wasn't happy, and neither was she.

I remember driving down the road one day, talking with Joey and telling her, "I'm pretty sure that the only way that this can work is if we are both willing to give everything up for the other person . . . our hopes and plans and dreams . . . if that's what it takes. If that means that my songwriting is getting in the way of our marriage, then I walk away and do something else. If it's your music, then you walk away. Whatever it takes. If we aren't willing to do that, and we put anything above our marriage, we are going to fail."

She just kept looking out the window, listening, then finally turned her head my way and said, "I'm sorry, but I'm not willing to give up my dreams for you."

And that was that. We were in a free fall. Sorta.

What actually happened was that our agendas went into a free fall. What she had planned fell apart. The record label didn't think she was ready to be a star and wanted her to sing in a smoky bar an hour away, five nights a week for the next six months. She told them no. And my agenda of Joey being a stay-at-home mom for the girls went away too. Neither of us got what we wanted.

Within six months Joey's record deal had fallen apart and disappeared. She was left brokenhearted, still working full-time at the horse vet clinic with no hope or prospect of her dreams ever coming true again. I had pulled the kids out of the mediocre schools they were in and was trying to homeschool them, all the while resenting Joey for not stepping in to help. I was disheartened and disillusioned. This whole marriage thing was turning out to be lose, lose, lose.

Mostly for the kids, though, I think.

Thirty-Eight

LOVE DOESN'T EXIST

Just before Joey and I started dating, Heidi had come to me and said she wanted to talk. She knew I had just broken up with a girl that she liked and was going to start dating this new girl named Joey. She had heard me telling other people that something inside me was telling me that this was magic.

She'd had enough. She was now fifteen and wise to the world—at least to mine.

"It doesn't exist, Dad," she said to me that night in her bedroom. "The kinda love that you write songs about . . . it isn't real. It sounds nice, and I'm sure for some people it happens, but not for us. And not for you." She went on to tell me that the girl I had been dating was nice. She was fun. And maybe that was enough. That I should stay with her so we could be happy for a while and not have all the drama we'd had in the past.

I completely understood where she was coming from. I was the one who had drug them through all the things they'd been through. But I also knew that God had been working on me, on my character. Preparing me for something great, maybe. So I told her that she might be right. "Maybe this one will turn out like the others, but maybe it won't," I said. "Just watch and see where this goes. I believe that this thing with Joey might be magic. A God thing. I might be wrong," I said. "But let's just watch and see. That's all I ask."

She had watched, and she was watching still. Both of the girls were watching us cry and hurt and hearing us argue and plead with each other, and with God, for some answers. Now we were in a worse place than before. Married and lonely. Together and apart. Committed to nothing, really.

Joey and I were at a low point. There was nothing left of us or our hopes. We were both empty. We couldn't cry any more tears, and there was nothing left to say that we hadn't said. But still, we were together. We hadn't gone anywhere, or threatened to. It had been about a year since we'd said our vows, and we had hung in there. That was about all I could say. But it was something.

From that low point, God began to build something. Something very special. Something bigger than us, bigger than our separate hopes and dreams. He took our agendas from us and gave us His. To love Him. To trust Him. To serve Him. And each other. And we did. Little by little, we grew closer. First to Him and then to each other. Our wills gave way to His will. And I remember one day looking up and seeing my wife—*really* seeing her. She was in her garden, picking asparagus that she'd grown, with chickens running around the yard and an amazing meal on the table. And I remember thinking, *She is incredible. My wife is amazing.*

And she was. I hadn't really known that before. Not really. I hadn't wanted it. I think I had a vision of what I thought an amazing wife would be, but it was nothing compared to what I was now seeing in Joey. This woman was true. And honest as the day is long. Hardworking and humble. So humble. It's like I woke up one day and realized that I had won the lottery. Out of all the men in the world, God had called the six numbers I held, and the prize was Joey.

Within another year or so, we were the most in-love two people you've ever met. Our empty cup now runneth over. It poured out of our hearts onto each other, then splashed all over anyone else who was near us. It was sickening almost. For the first time it hit me: I, Rory Feek, was married to a great woman. A really, really great woman. And, for some reason, Joey thought the same of me. How did that happen? I don't know—it just did.

And through it all, my girls had been watching. They'd seen the hard times we'd had. And they'd seen us stick it out and get on our knees and turn our tears into prayers and our prayers into smiles and laughter. For the first time, they saw their father in love. Truly in love. And they saw a woman honoring their daddy. The thing that I think they wanted to see most of all.

They are watching still. Grown now, but watching. Learning from us. How to live truly loving someone and how to love someone even when living isn't an option anymore. That has been such a gift to me. To know that after all those years of getting it wrong, of giving them bad examples and images to look at, we were able to give them some good ones.

I've learned that it's never too late to start over. Never too late to impact someone in a good way. Every day is a new day—the start of a new and better story.

Thirty-Nine

A GREEN HEART

Joey can grow onions and tomatoes, potatoes and zucchini, and squash and peppers and corn 'til they're coming out your ears. That, and love. That's what she really grows best.

Joey had a gift of seeing things simply. Black and white, right and wrong. No gray areas, not really. As I've mentioned, she didn't really know that she saw things that way, or understand what it was she was doing . . . but I did. I could see it, analyze it, understand it all . . . but couldn't do it. Joey could just do it, and she managed to skip all the steps in between. It was another one of her many gifts from God.

—⁓—

Each year in the late winter, Joey would start ordering seeds. She'd pull out her dog-eared catalogs, and her bookmarked seed-savers exchange website link, and spend days preparing, then placing orders for all the things she wanted to grow in her garden. The things she wanted to put on our table, in our freezer, and on our pantry shelves. It would still be cold outside, but you'd think spring was already here by how excited she'd get about it. She'd ask me if I thought we should get the Burgundy Red or Black Beauty beans or the Indian-head sweet or bread-and-butter corn. I never could really tell much of a difference in how they all tasted, but I'd pretend that I did and do my best to help her decide. Joey was passionate about her garden. About raising good food to feed her family.

It was a lot of work. Like I said, I'm a little more analytical about things, and it didn't take much figuring to realize that it's not only faster and easier but also cheaper to just head to Kroger to buy the food to cook for dinner, rather than grow it. Mostly because *growing* is a complicated word. *Growing* actually means preparing, planting, weeding, and watering the seeds and the soil they grow in. Then a bunch more work starts once you've done that. Besides the picking and harvesting, there's the peeling and the cutting and the canning, the shucking and the boiling and the bagging, and the freezing. All that so you can do the cooking. The math never really added up to me. But for Joey it did.

And it didn't just add up to her; it was super one-sided. The garden outweighed the grocery store any day. And every day. My wife understood that there are things you cannot put a price on, and there's a huge difference between time wasted and time spent. The amount of time that Joey was in her garden, or doing things in and around it, were outside of time. Outside of money. They existed on a different plane. "How do you put a price on your family's health?" she would say. To know what she was feeding her children and husband was very important to Joey. And to know that she played a small part in the existence of that food was a big source of pride for her.

And she had a strong opinion about GMOs—genetically modified organisms. She wouldn't go near or serve her family anything that wasn't non-GMO. For her it wasn't a government or big-business thing—although neither she nor I have much trust in either—it was a nature thing. GMOs aren't right or natural, and a lot of research out there says that for all the good they can do in the short-term, all that modifying of what God Himself provided for us is doing irreversible damage to our bodies and our health. There weren't many things that Joey would get on a soapbox about, but that was one of them. That and immunizations. But I'll save that for a different chapter—in probably a different book someday—about raising something even more precious to Joey than the garden full of vegetables that she loved.

Besides her garden, Joey always had chickens too. We'd keep a dozen in the henhouse for eggs each morning, and she'd get fifty or a hundred day-old chicks each spring to raise for meat-birds for our freezer.

My wife didn't like to read much. Not really. Reading to her was the same thing as watching a movie. It meant going to sleep. But she did love reading the latest book or article by Joel Salatin from Swoope, Virginia, the self-proclaimed "lunatic farmer" she heard about. About how he moves his chickens from spot to spot each day in a homemade chicken tractor so they can have new grass to peck and new soil, around the garden, to leave droppings. Joey loved learning about homesteading and farming and simple living. And the more old-fashioned and commonsense, the better. I bought her a brand-new tiller a few years ago, but she continued using the one her mama had given her. The one that would beat you to death as you moved up and down the rows. It would turn the soil over just fine, but it would also turn your arms and body to mush because it was so old and rickety. Joey loved it, though, because it had history. Her mama had used it and probably some other mamas before that.

I have two freezers full of things Joey has grown. Enough to last a good while. Probably a year or two would be my guess. We've been pulling some green beans and other vegetables out for dinner the last couple of evenings, and though the bags say 2014 or 2015, the food tastes like it just came straight out of the garden. I know she would love that she's still providing for us, even now. And I love still being able to "taste" Joey here at our table, even though she's no longer in the chair next to mine.

Another part of me wants to leave them there. Those bags. The vegetables and fruit of Joey's hard labor. Leave them in the freezer and not eat them. I don't want to walk out to the mudroom one day and open the freezer door to find all the bags she carefully filled and dated are gone. Or worse yet, find the freezer filled with nothing but bags of chicken from Kroger or Whole Foods and no sign of Joey or the foods that were most important to her.

As I look out the window and type this, Joey's garden is full of life. Life has begun to spring from the seeds Indiana and Hopie and I and some friends planted this spring, with hopes of keeping our table filled with Joey's beliefs in healthy living and eating. To honor her. To see if, just maybe, in doing that, one of our older girls or the little one will pick up Joey's passion for the garden and run with it. Make it her own.

One thing I know is that the love Joey planted here will not die. It continues blooming and growing. I see it, feel it, everywhere. It's in our hearts and in the smiles on our faces and in the hands that I shake and the people I meet when I am dropping Indy off at school. Her love is everywhere. Planted in the life she lived. That we lived. And the story that we have told and are still telling. That kind of love takes root in the hearts of others, of people we will never meet. At least, this side of heaven.

Joey would love that. To know that she's made a small difference in the world. And a big difference in mine.

Forty

CHANGING LIVES ONE SIP AT A TIME

I often say, "All the best things happen around a cup of coffee." I especially say that to my buddies Chris and Matt who own Muletown Coffee—a little chain of coffee shops nearby in Columbia, Tennessee.

But it's true. As I mentioned, my first date with Joey was having coffee at Stan's Truck Stop, and years later the idea for us to sing together would show itself over a cup of coffee on Edgehill Avenue, in Nashville. And then there's Marcy Jo's . . . the cup of coffee that spawned a million more cups of coffee.

—⁓—

Joey's record deal had evaporated a few years earlier, and with it went her dreams of getting the chance to be a singer. To follow in her hero Dolly Parton's big, little footsteps.

Joey had gone back to working as a vet assistant at Equine Medical, now the Tennessee Equine Hospital. She loved her job, but part of her wanted more. We had been married for four years by this time, and she was starting to come to the conclusion that maybe music wasn't in the cards for her. That was hard for her to swallow. It was why she had moved to Nashville and why she had been born. Or, at least, for her it felt that way. But even she could read the signs. God had been closing doors before she could even knock on them. It was beyond disheartening.

Still she trusted Him, that He had a plan. And she laid her disappointment at His feet daily. So when she and Marcy and I were having coffee one afternoon at our kitchen table and Marcy said, "You know, Jo, you and I should open up a little cafe in that little building down the road," Joey thought about it for a minute, about all the doors that had been closed in her face, about the way our marriage had worked out wonderfully—even though we were scared and disappointed at first—and she said, "Okay, let's do it." And they did.

We did, actually. I was recruited to do the plumbing and the electrical. That's why Marcy Jo's still has leaky pipes and water pouring all over the floor more than every now and then. They decided to do it in October 2006, I think. And they opened for business in mid-January 2007. They called it Marcy Jo's Mealhouse & Bakery. Marcy for Marcy, and the Jo for Joey. Marcy would do the cooking and run the kitchen, and Joey would do the baking and wait on tables.

My wife was nervous as could be about it. "I'm used to horses, not people," she would say. "I don't think I'm good with people." But she was. She was a natural. My wife's love language is "service," and you don't get much more "service-y" than slinging eggs and coffee to customers. And not only was she good at it, she loved it. And she loved the people, and they loved her. The first customer through the door was an older cowboy named Danny Smith. By the time his belly was full, Danny, Marcy, and Joey were fast friends. The next time he came in, he was carrying a new air conditioner, still in the box, from Home Depot. "To help keep the girls cool in that hotter-than-Hades kitchen," he said. With the gift of that A/C, Danny stole my wife's heart and the admiration of those girls for a lifetime. "He is a good man," Joey told me when she got home that night. "All our neighbors are good people," she said.

I remember sitting at the top of the driveway with Joey about a month after they opened the cafe and her standing beside her truck in tears. Not the bad kind either. They were tears of pride because it was the first thing she'd ever done, she said, that was hers. The first thing that she'd ever owned, that she was part of building. And it changed her. It totally changed who she was and what mattered to her. She let the music go. She didn't need it anymore, not the way she did before. She could finally open her hand and give it to Him. Completely.

And I think it was then, and only then, that He could give it to her. The music. The dream she'd always wanted. To sing on a stage and have a million people watching and hearing her.

He was about to give it to her.

Only because now she didn't need it.

That's when He does it sometimes. And He'll do it in a way that you never expected.

That's what He did with us, anyway.

Forty-One

NOTHING MATTERS

The things you think matter? They don't. And the things you think mean nothing? They're the ones that change everything.

I've seen it happen again and again. In my life and in others. This book is filled with them. Or at least it should be if I get it right. And this was one of those times—when it shouldn't have mattered, but it did. When I thought nothing was happening, but it was. A day that I thought was insignificant, but it wasn't. It was life-changing. Two lives changing. Joey's and mine.

Like all days that change everything, this was just a regular, ordinary Thursday. I had a songwriting appointment with a guy at the farm. No big deal. He was a friend of a friend. I didn't know him, and honestly, I wanted to cancel it. Stay at home and do something else more important. Less important. Whatever. But I didn't cancel it. Thank God.

John Bollinger was from Montana. His buddy Dave was someone I'd met a few years earlier, and Dave had asked me to write with John, and so I'd told him I would. And now John was here, at the farmhouse, and we were spending the day together, trying to write a song. John was a super guy. I knew right away that I liked him. Very funny and talented and humble. It's my favorite character in people. Humility. In myself too. Or, at least, I hope it is.

We spent the morning working on a song, and then at lunchtime I took him down the road to Marcy Jo's. I explained to him that I had recently won the lottery because I not only got to be served by that pretty waitress who was refilling our tea glasses, but I was sleeping with her too. He thought that was funny. I introduced him to Joey, and we stayed for a long time visiting. He asked lots of questions about our lives and our little restaurant and farm. He and I had fried chicken or whatever special they were serving that day. Then we went back and wrote a little more, and he headed out. That was it.

But that wasn't it.

John called me on my cell a week or so later. He wanted to know if Joey and I could come to Nashville and meet with him for coffee. He wanted to run something by us, and it needed to be soon. I thought it strange, but I told him we'd be there.

The next day, John sat across from Joey and me at a little coffee shop just off Music Row. He told us that besides being a songwriter, he was also a band leader for a TV show called *Nashville Star*. He said he knew a lot of people in that industry, and a new show was about to go into production by the people who do *American Idol*, and they were looking for America's next great country duo. And he said he told them about us.

I said, "John, what are you talking about? Joey's a singer, and I'm a songwriter, but we don't sing together. We're not a duo." He just smiled.

Then he said, "I've been doing this a long time and have met a lot of people. And you don't realize it, but you and Joey—you're the real deal." He told us he thought it would be a good idea for us to audition for the show. I didn't think it was.

On the way to our truck, Joey asked me if I'd do it. For her. She knew that I embarrassed easily, and one of my worst fears was seeing myself in pictures and, even worse, on TV. But I could tell that this opportunity meant a lot to her. She was now thirty-two years old, and that's old for women who are trying to have a singing career.

Against my better judgment, I told her I would. And that would turn out to be one of the best bad decisions I would ever make. Period.

As nervous and afraid as I was for myself, I believed in Joey. I had been saying for years, "It would be a tragedy if the world never got a chance to hear my wife sing." I knew she had a gift and never really understood why God hadn't opened the right door for her dreams. But He hadn't. And I would soon find out why.

He had a bigger plan. He always does.

John said they needed to see something on video of Joey and me singing together. Just a song or two. I had a better idea. My cousin Aaron and I went to Best Buy and bought a little consumer video camera and made a seven-minute video that didn't just show us singing a couple of songs but also told our story. I wanted the producers, or whoever would be watching it, to see how special my wife was and to know a little more about us than how well we sang together or what we looked like.

Joey did her part too. She baked a pan of pecan sticky buns and delivered them to the producer along with the DVD that Aaron and I had made. A day or two later we found out that we were in. Way in. I wouldn't know how far that little video and those sticky buns would carry us until months later, but one thing was clear. The producers saw something unique in Joey and me and thought that the people who tuned in to watch the show would too.

We went all the way to the finals of CMT's *Can You Duet* television show, and that led to a record deal for Joey and me. And the chance to perform all over the country and halfway around the world, sell hundreds of thousands of albums, make music videos and television commercials, and, ultimately, have our very own television show that we would film at home in the big red barn beside our farmhouse. But the most amazing part of it is that it happened to *us*—not just to Joey. That in itself is a miracle. We had *never* considered singing together. And even when the doors that had closed for my wife started opening up for us as a husband-and-wife duo, I was still skeptical. I had never seen anything like it in the music business, and I had been in it a long time. Never heard of anything that wonderful and sweet and genuine happening to another couple the way it did for us.

And that is a wonderful gift. Not just because we got to experience it but because it was very clear that it wasn't something that we, or I, did. It was magic. Only God could've pulled it off. Joey and I stood on that stage each night, in awe of the opportunity to be there. To be there together.

It became clear that when Joey heard or felt that still small voice telling her "He's the one" at the Bluebird Cafe all those years ago, God didn't just have a beautiful love in store for us. He had that and more in mind. A love story that He could share with others. A platform that would become bigger than words and music. Bigger than the songs we were singing.

I believe—no, I know—He purposely let all those doors close for Joey and her heart be broken because He had something in store for her. Something bigger and better than what she, or I, dreamed of.

And it all started with that one appointment I almost canceled.

He made something extraordinary out of the ordinary.

I love that.

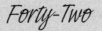

MONEY

I never knew how much money we had. Never. We could've been broke or been millionaires, and I would've had no way of knowing.

Joey handles the money in our family. At least, she always did. Early on in our marriage, I had proven myself not to be very good with money, at least in the managing of it. So she took it over and made the rules. She managed how much came in and how much went out and knew what we could afford and what we couldn't. I was on a need-to-know basis when it came to our money situation. Not that she didn't trust me with it; it was just easier that way. And better.

My wife was very good with our family's finances, mostly because money didn't mean anything to her, I think. When I say it didn't mean anything, I don't mean that she didn't care about it or that she blew through it like it was going out of style. It wasn't like that. What I'm saying is that money didn't mean to her what it means to most other people. It didn't mean happiness or power. And it wasn't a goal of hers to have a lot of it. Or to have a big stockpile of it. She only wanted enough. That was all she needed. All we needed.

Joey was old-fashioned when it came to money. She was against us having debt. And when we did, she wanted to pay it off, or down, as soon as possible. Like me, she didn't have much growing up. But unlike me, her folks had instilled in her a very strong work ethic and a sense of pride when it came to paying back what you owed right away. And of being frugal. Joey wasn't a shopper. She didn't enjoy going store to store, looking for the next thing to make her feel better about herself or the life she was living. Buying things didn't make her happy. For her, she only wanted what we needed. Nothing more, nothing less.

I think she had a keen sense about our human nature to always want more, no matter how much we already have. And she wanted us to be better than that. To stay off that empty treadmill, and others like it, that most of society seems to find itself on these days.

Some couples try to keep separate bank accounts. Hers and his. Make it so that a portion of their money is for him to do what he wants, and some is hers to spend however she chooses. Joey didn't like that idea. Everything was ours. And it all went into the same pot. If there was something I wanted or needed, I would just ask her. And she would tell me if we could buy it or not. I didn't always like her answer, but I always respected it. I knew it was coming from a place of love, not a place of control or power. Sometimes when I knew we were doing well and I wanted something and she told me no, it wasn't because we couldn't afford it. It was because she knew I didn't need it. Or even more, she knew it wouldn't be good for me. Or for us.

Us . . . our marriage . . . keeping it solid and secure was always the goal. And she and I both were smart enough to realize that money is usually one of the things that makes or breaks marriages. We strived to not let that be the case for us.

Joey also knew our kids were watching. If we had an emptiness inside of us that we were using money to fill, then they would most likely grow up to do the same thing. She wanted them to at least see that their parents were trying to take a different path, even if in the end they had to learn it the hard way. The girls are older now and making their way in the world. And I can honestly say they are both much better with money than I was at their ages. Much, much better. That is all Joey's doing. I wish I could say it is mine, but it isn't.

And lastly, Joey knew that I was watching. I know that she never had any idea that this time would come and I would be the one making the financial decisions for our family, but she knew I was beside her all those years, paying attention to the decisions she made on our behalf. And I was watching. I saw the difference that "doing the best right thing" makes. And I do my best to keep that going.

During the almost fourteen years of our marriage, I would find out that I could do pretty well at making money—but taking care of it and being responsible with it were never my strong suits. Thank God Joey taught me to be better. To see money for what it is: a blessing. A blessing that God gives us that we can use to bless others.

Forty-Three

RHYMES WITH TEX

I think there's some statistic somewhere that says that if it's not money that does in a marriage, it's sex. And I can understand that. Sex is like money, only a thousand, million times more powerful.

C. S. Lewis calls selfishness and pride the great sin. But I think sex may be running in a close second. It's a monster. If you polled a thousand men on the street right now and asked them what they are thinking about, 995 of them would say sex. They would if you could get them to be honest. But you won't. Men can't be honest about sex. That subject's too hard for them to talk about. To be honest about. I get it. I'm one of them. Men. We're wired weird.

Even when we're married and we're happy, we're thinking about it. Even when we just had it, we want more of it. Well, after a nap we do. It's a strange thing. And I, for one, do not have it figured out. But my wife Joey did. At least, she had a good grasp on a lot of it.

It was easier for her. Easier to understand men, I think. Most women walk around throwing their hands up in the air when it comes to men and their desires and needs. But not Joey. She understood men and how they're wired, or at least she understood the man she was married to.

To her, it came down to nature. It wasn't me being weird; it was me being me. How God made me. How God made all of us. With wants and needs that are so deep inside of us that we can't think straight sometimes, and we let those needs do the thinking instead of our hearts or the brains in our heads.

Joey knew her husband was a man. And she was the woman God had given him. That was all the information she needed. For her, my needs were her needs. That was her job. Her blessing. It may not have been the job she wanted all the time, or even half or a quarter of the time, but it was hers just the same. She loved me. And she knew that for a man—at least this one—sex was one of the ways I needed her to express her love for me.

I can't tell you that our love life was perfect because it wasn't. It was like everyone else's. Amazing at times, with fireworks that lit up the bedroom sky, and strained at other times, with her on one side of our king-size bed and me on the other. Confused. Upset. Disappointed. Not understanding her and mostly feeling that she didn't understand me.

But we tried never to go to sleep angry with each other. And with few exceptions, we never did. We both knew the words "I'm sorry," and we raced each other to say them. Not at first. Early on, those two words were hard to say. But through the years we learned that was where the magic was. And we couldn't get our apologies out fast enough. We might not have always been able to work out our problems, but we tried not to take them to bed with us. To wake up with them still there in the morning. Each new day brought its own unique challenges without adding ones from a day that had already passed.

—⁂—

This is a subject that matters. That really, really matters. And like all things that scare us, there's really only one way to approach our fears. Head-on. That being said, Joey and I have always been very private when it comes to private matters. She would want me to say it without saying it. Or try to. Either way, it needs to be said. Especially to and for us men who have no one to go to for answers when it comes to this stuff. And we desperately need help. The world is bombarding us with images and information that show and tell us the opposite of what we actually need to hear: the honest truth.

I am no different from anyone else. Especially any other man. Except, maybe, I've failed more than most, and sex has been a big part of that failure for me. It's a key part of the wound that is deep in me, that is in most of us, and it is what has gotten me into trouble the most. It's where I have disappointed myself and others more times than I can count. It's what I stay the most confused and conflicted about. And it's also where I have found the most healing and sense of accomplishment in my marriage.

I have never cheated on my wife. I know that's not a big deal for a lot of people to say, but it is. For me it is. I have been true to her. And I am so very proud of that.

When Joey was in hospice and nearing the end, her sisters gathered around me and asked me how I was doing. They said, "This must be very hard on you . . . very tough on you, physically. All these months. The past year and a half." I knew what they were asking. And I told them it was. But then again, it wasn't. I was committed to their sister. And I don't mean in only an "I love her" sort of way. I'm talking about a commitment that I made to her. That I made to myself.

When we got married, I decided there would be no one else but Joey. And that meant no one else. Not in real life and not in my head. I committed to not allowing myself to experience the greatest expression of love that a person can feel without my bride being with me. Not ever. Not once. And that was a big, big deal. She didn't ask for that. Or require it. I wanted to give it. To see if I could do it. If I could be that true to someone. To Joey. To see if I could not only be true to her but also true to myself. Committed to myself for her. And I was. To the end of the line.

When you come from where I came from, from who I was, and you have the undeserved opportunity to love a woman like Joey . . . it was the least I could do.

And I believe that it made a difference. There was never a time when I didn't want my wife. Never. And I believe my desire to honor Joey and her desire to honor me are part of why God has given us such a beautiful marriage and love story. I don't just believe it; I know it.

Where do I go from here? What does the future hold when it comes to these things for me? I don't know.

All I know is that I was hers. True to her.

I am still hers.

Forty-Four

THE NAME GAME

Feek? That's the stupidest name I've ever heard.

For years I didn't use my last name. For lots of reasons.

First off, it was a name that was easy for kids to make fun of in school, and as I got older, it was much the same.

Secondly, when I was growing up, my father was a bit of a rounder, and though I know he meant well, he didn't leave much of a legacy for our last name. I had no idea where the name came from or even where the people in past generations who used it came from. So when I moved to Nashville in '95 and was about to sign a publishing deal, as the lady handed me the pen to sign—and potentially etch my name in stone on albums and CDs if I ever had any success—I asked her, "Should I use my last name Feek or my middle name Lee?"

She kinda laughed and said, "Feek? That's the stupidest name I've ever heard. Definitely use Lee."

So I became Rory Lee, songwriter. For the first few years in town, everyone knew me that way. And when I had my first hit song, that's the name on the back of the CD.

But then Joey and I got married, and the name became an issue. It had actually become a concern a couple of years before that, as I stood at the end of our driveway after buying the farmhouse, trying to decide whether to use *Lee* on the mailbox or *Feek*. I pondered that one for a long time and finally settled on *Lee*.

When we stood at the altar and took those vows together, Joey also vowed to take my name and wear it proudly. But she asked me if she could continue being Joey Martin for her music career. I was leery of her doing that and told her so. She just listened and didn't really say anything. Sometime during our honeymoon, though, the subject of her using her maiden name came to a head. We were talking about her music career, and I told her again that I thought she should use Feek and not Martin. The main reason I felt that way was because I was insecure about losing her to the music business or someone else, and I secretly thought that saddling her with my name would let people know that she was taken. (She had to be . . . or why else would she have a name like that?) It's embarrassing to admit that now. But it's true.

Somewhere in the middle of our blissful honeymoon and arguments over careers, kids, life, and a million other things we hadn't worked out before saying I do, she said again, "I will gladly take your name and wear it proudly every day of my life, but I would like to be able to go by Joey Martin for my dad and my family when I'm singing."

The conversation got heated, and I think there might have been some tears involved. I put my foot down and said, "No. It's not right."

Then she looked at me and said, "How can you say that, when *you* don't even use your own last name?"

I hadn't thought of that. But she had, and rightly so.

I told her that was different, but I knew it wasn't. She had me cornered. I caved and gave my blessing for her to use her maiden name, and we dropped the subject. For years we never mentioned it again. Not once.

But then one day in a songwriting appointment with Allen Shamblin, the name problem showed up again. Allen had cowritten Bonnie Raitt's "I Can't Make You Love Me" and Miranda Lambert's "The House That Built Me" and was an exceptionally profound thinker and man of faith. He started telling me about a recent trip back home to Texas that he'd taken and how their local church had a revival that shook the town to the core. People were coming to Christ, and change was happening in the congregation like never before. It had all started with the pastor standing in front of the congregation one morning and facing his greatest fear. He reached up and removed the toupee he had worn for years. Allen said everyone knew the pastor wore one, but no one ever said anything out of respect. They could sense that it was a big deal for him. But when he found the courage to get out from under the shame that he'd been carrying around, it caused a chain reaction in the lives of the people sitting in the pews. It was a great story, and I think we wrote a song about it, or part of one. But afterward, I drove home that evening, deep in thought.

A few hours later, after the kids went to bed, Joey and I sat on the bed together, and I started weeping. She didn't understand what was wrong, so I told her. "I have to start using my last name," I said. "It's killing me." I told her how I was leaving no legacy for our kids, and that now that they were teenagers, people didn't know whether they were Heidi and Hopie Lee or Feek. Not only did I not have any pride in my last name; I wasn't instilling any in them. And that was wrong. Joey knew it was a big deal to me. We cried together and prayed together. I nervously told God that I needed His help to face my fear, and though I would probably be undoing all the progress I'd made building a name for myself in Nashville as a songwriter, I was putting it in His hands. I believed that something good would come of it.

From that moment on I started introducing myself as Rory Feek and claiming what was rightly mine. The funny thing is that no one cared. I mean, no one. It was all in my head. As a matter of fact, a few weeks later I told the story to one of my industry friends, and he said, "Man, Rory Feek is an awesome name." He actually liked it better. And so I started liking it better too.

Before long I found that God took that commitment I made and lifted my name higher than it had ever been lifted before. Amazing things have come to Rory Feek that Rory Lee would've never dreamed possible. And I believe it's because I made that change and faced that fear. I learned that on the other side of fear is joy and blessing and, even more so, peace.

Forty-Five

TEN PERCENT

I've never been a good tither. It just didn't make any sense to me.

First off, I was always poor. And I couldn't give 10 percent of what's already not enough to pay my bills. I could, but it wouldn't be smart. The second thing was, even if I'd had money, I certainly wasn't going to trust the church with it. Not a certain church in particular, but all of 'em. The whole darn lot. It was hard to see the difference between Brother Bobby at the local Church of Christ, with an attendance of fifty on a good Sunday, passing the hat around, and someone who was on my TV in a three-thousand-dollar suit, begging for my money so he could upgrade to the latest luxury jet to fly to his winter home in Cancun.

I didn't trust any of it. But when I'd get to feeling generous or exceptionally guilty, I would drop a twenty in the plate, instead of the three ones or handful of coins that I usually put in on Sundays, if I gave anything at all. I think Joey felt a similar way too. She never said so, but she also never asked me for a calculator to figure out what 10 percent of our weekly checks was. We were apathetic to the whole thing.

A few years into our marriage, though, that changed. And again, it happened in the most unexpected of ways.

I was in a meeting north of Nashville with a big merchandise company, Richards & Southern. The owner, Terry, was taking me all around, giving me the tour of the buildings and telling me how they had grown it from a little postcard company that his daddy had started years ago to a multimillion-dollar merchandising business with big artists like Kenny Chesney and George Strait as clients. But as we walked into one particular room and he was in the middle of telling me how these new machines they'd bought had revolutionized his company and helped his profits skyrocket, he stopped midsentence and stopped walking too. He looked back at me and said, "No, Rory, that's actually not true. That's not what happened."

Then he told me a different story. About how he and his wife, Sheri, hadn't been going to church much, but in the eighties they had started to go more, and he had been convicted to start tithing, to give 10 percent of everything he made. And how it was a terrible idea and he thought it would bankrupt them, but he did it anyway, and instead of ruining his business, the next year it grew. So he gave more, and the next year it grew twice as big as before, and pretty soon the 10 percent he was giving to the church each month was more than he had made in a whole year before he had started tithing. He finished by saying, "That's really how it happened, Rory. That's how it's happening now." He told me how good it feels to give, that it's not really his money anyway. It's God's. He's just getting a part of it back. Terry was honest and said he wasn't sure what the church does with it, but that's not for him to know. He was just learning to give with a cheerful heart, and it had made all the difference in his business and in his marriage.

Now, Terry didn't know me from Adam. He didn't know that I was a new Christian, struggling, still trying to find my way with trusting God with my life and my money. He didn't have to know that, I guess. He just said what was on his heart. Little did he know it was what I needed to hear, when I needed to hear it.

I came home and told Joey the story that Terry had told me and about the joy that I saw in his eyes and in his company. Joey and I talked a long time about it. We weren't in a position to give away 10 percent of what we had. At the time we only had enough to pay our bills. But we prayed about it and decided to start giving, to begin setting aside the first 10 percent of all we made and giving it to the One who had ultimately given it to us. What He did with it was for Him to decide. We would find a church, or a few of them, and start giving. And so we did.

That first check was hard to write. It was only a hundred bucks or so, but it put Joey and me in the red, and that was scary. But something about it felt so good. To give. To give without desiring anything in return. The next month we gave again. Then the next and the next. And through it all, we always seemed to have enough. Enough to get by and enough to continue to give. But then something strange began to happen. The pool of money that we were giving from began to grow. Within a year the monthly income that we had used to calculate our 10 percent tithe for the first check was less than what was now our monthly tithe. It was incredible. Not that tithing is meant to be a way to increase your income; it isn't. But don't be surprised if it works out that way sometimes. It's again how God does things. His math. His logic never makes sense on paper, but it works in real life.

There have been times since then that we have had tougher spells, when money is tight, and there have been periods in our marriage with great abundance. But through it all, Joey and I have tried to remain faithful. To give God what is rightly His. At times, we give even more than what is required, and it has been our honor. We've seen the fruit of tithing, and you can't put a number on it. So don't even try.

Just take out your checkbook and give a portion of what you make away. To a church. To a stranger. To someone you love. To someone you don't like.

Just give it to God. He'll use it to change someone's life.

And yours.

Forty-Six

ON THE SAME PAGE

Joey and I have rarely ever argued or raised our voices at each other. Even when times were really trying, like in that first year or so of our marriage, we didn't get mad and yell or argue with each other much. We talked. We reasoned. And we hurt. And we cried some tears. But what we did most was pray.

Sometimes we prayed together. We held hands and lifted our problems up to Someone and something bigger and smarter than us. And sometimes we prayed on our own. I have no doubt that in those early days Joey spent the time driving to work in her truck in deep conversation and prayer with God about our troubles. Asking, begging Him to help. To help me understand her pain and her to understand mine. And I did my share of praying too. I still do. It doesn't always look like prayer. It looks more like cooking dinner or mowing the lawn. But it's still prayer. Me thinking about Him and what it is He wants. Trying to get the focus off of myself and on to where it's supposed to be—on Him.

———✕———

For Joey and me, it was about being on the same page or getting on the same page if we weren't. And that's not always easy. It's almost impossible for a lot of people, I think, because they're working out of different books.

Coming from a place that is different from the other person's. It makes sense, too, because we all come from different places. Different backgrounds and families. And we have all read different books and been given different bits of wisdom that we try to draw from when we can't figure things out on our own. Those things are good, but I'm not sure they'll get the job done when the going gets really tough.

Joey and I were both clear that there's only one place and one book that we should be working out of: the Bible. On the pages of the Old and New Testaments were the answers we needed. Whether we knew it or not, almost always, it was our unhappiness with ourselves that made us unhappy with each other. And most of the unhappiness was something spiritual that we were struggling with. We were wrestling with God and taking it out on each other.

From the very beginning, we understood that we needed Him to be the head of our household if this was ever going to be a home. We knew that left to our own devices we would mess it up. We would ruin the beautiful thing God had given us. My selfishness, or hers, or both, would. But if we could keep things in perspective—that our marriage and the life we were living were gifts—then maybe, just maybe, we could make it and not end up on the bad end of some statistic on marriages today.

We chose a single verse to live by and love by when we got married: "As for me and my house, we will serve the LORD" (Joshua 24:15). It was printed on the napkins for our wedding reception and even deeper in our hearts as we started our marriage. Joey and I took it to mean: "It's not about what I want; it's about what He wants." And not he, meaning me, the man . . . but He, the big He. God the Father. We both knew that the best thing we could do for our marriage and our children was serve Him. If we did that . . . if we did it right, then when people looked at our relationship and saw Joey serving me and me serving her, what they'd really be seeing was us serving Him.

My wife was always inherently better at this than me. She was the great servant in our house. It was in her DNA. I was a novice compared to her. But Joey inspired me daily to be better. To give more and love more and to think of myself less. She inspires me still. I have a long way to go to catch up to her level of servanthood, but I strive for it.

And I know it's possible because I've seen it in action. In her.

Forty-Seven

BABY CRAZY

Y ou wanna have a baby? Are you crazy?"

I've always loved babies. Always. My wife knows this about me. We could be at an airport, rushing to get to our gate so we don't miss our plane, and she might see me veer off and go say hi to a toddler who's learning to stand by his mama and their bags. Or ask a man how old the baby in his arms is. It's just how I'm wired. I'm crazy about those little eyes and fingers and toes.

Joey was exactly the opposite. She felt nothing. When I would see the cutest little face and smile on a baby, she would see diapers and dishes and sleepless nights and pain. Pain from pushing. The only labor my wife wanted to go through is the kind where she is getting her hands dirty to do it. She was scared of babies. I mean, all-out frightened at the thought of having them anywhere near her. In the first ten years we were married, she wouldn't pick up or hold a baby, even if it was one of her sisters' children.

Joey made it clear early in our marriage that we were not going to have more children. She would take my name, be my wife, and serve and love me with all of her heart and soul, 'til death do us part, but she was not going to have a baby with me.

That worried me. For her. I had spent enough of my life trying to control things and "have it my way" to know that usually whatever it is that we refuse to give to God is probably *the one thing* He wants from us.

I was afraid that might be the case with this for Joey. I told her so, too, a few times. Bad idea. That was a sure way to get into a big argument. Not only was she *not* going to have a baby; she wasn't even gonna have this conversation. So I just played along and waited and watched to see what would come of it.

It was a strange thing, seeing Joey hold on so tightly to something. I knew my wife well, and I knew how much she loved God. And me. So for her to make something so off-limits was hard for me to understand. But I tried to. I didn't push her. Besides, I already had two kids and knew that I had been blessed so much more than I deserved. I could not, and would not, ask God for more. But that didn't stop me from joking with Joey about it some. Our bus driver, Russell, and I would kid her about babies and how life would be if we had one, and she would play along until she got tired of playing, and then she'd shut it down. Russ and I would know we'd stepped over the line.

That went on for years. Joey insisting on having her way and not considering any other option. The other strange thing about that was it was literally the only thing about Joey that was out of character for her— inconsistent with who she was and what she was about. Every fiber in her being was about the good things in life. The simple things. Things like faith. And family. She was all about that. But not starting one.

A few years into our marriage, I started to get the feeling that the baby thing was going to be an issue. Not with me but with God. That there might come a time when He would require her to do the one thing she didn't want to do. Give the one thing she didn't want to give. And finally, it happened. Our baby Indiana.

Our little blessing happened because of all our blessings. Joey came to realize, over time, that God had blessed her and me greatly in our marriage. That all of her dreams had come true and then some. She was living a life blessed beyond her wildest dreams. And how could she withhold anything from Him? From me, if that's what He wanted? And so she came to me one day in 2012, about ten years into our marriage, and said, "I'm ready."

She said she was ready to give God everything. Even the part that scared her the most. Getting pregnant and having a baby. I asked her if she really wanted to have a child, and she said, "No . . . but even more than that, I want what God wants." She went on to say that it hurt her to think about how greatly God had blessed us and how tightly she had been holding on to her fear and she wanted to face it. To trust Him and give Him all of herself, completely. Once and for all.

I knew how scary that was for Joey. I wasn't even sure that I wanted another child. I mean, of course I did, in one way, because I love children and would love to be able to have and raise one with Joey. To share in that together, after all the years of having to do it on my own before she came along. But another part of me knew that I was older. Almost forty-eight then, and set in my ways. A lot of men that age are already having grandbabies. Maybe I was too old to have another little one running around my feet. But none of that mattered, compared to Joey facing her fears. If she could be faithful and trust God in this, I surely could. So I put my worries and thoughts aside completely and said, "Okay, let's see what happens."

Joey got pregnant about a year later.

I remember the day she told me. It was Father's Day, and I was working in the milk house on our property. The milking machines are long gone, but I have a desk in there now, and it's where I write songs and edit video on large-screen monitors. Joey knocked on the door and came in and handed me a Father's Day card and a little box that was wrapped in a bow. And she was so, so sweet. I read the card and then opened the box. Inside was a little plastic strip that had two pink lines on it. I looked up at her, not believing what I was seeing. "You're gonna be a daddy again," she said with a great big smile. "Happy Father's Day, honey." And we both broke down crying.

I pulled her down onto my lap, and we held each other and cried. I couldn't believe it. Neither could she. A million things went through my mind and hers. We talked and laughed and cried and celebrated, and then we did what we always did for all the big and small things in our life—we got down on our knees and held hands and prayed. We prayed a prayer of thanks and of awe and wonder, and we asked God to keep Joey and the baby safe and to give us hearts full of love and joy for the new season of life we were about to enter. That we would trust Him completely with this child, and with our lives, which were about to change because of this new addition to our family.

We had no way of knowing the joy and the sadness that moment and prayer would usher in. All we knew was that my wife had been faithful. That she had trusted God, and that would be our plan in the future.

His will and not ours.

Forty-Eight

ALMOND EYES

She has the prettiest little almond eyes. We named her Indiana. Indiana Boon Feek. And she is a gift, straight from heaven.

We were in bed one evening not long after we found out Joey was pregnant, and I had my iPad, trying to show her a film called *Babies* that I'd seen a couple of years before on Netflix, but I couldn't find it. Instead, we came across a documentary called *The Business of Being Born*, and we pushed play. An hour later my wife had gone from being scared of having a baby to wanting to have one at home with a midwife and no medicine. It was crazy. And awesome.

Everything about having a baby at home appealed to Joey. It is the way women have been doing it for thousands of years. It's all-natural, without chemicals and medicine running through the mama's or the baby's veins, and it's hard. The good kind of hard. Joey liked that kind of struggle. The kind where there is a reason for it. A higher purpose. And the second she heard about and came to understand that she could have a baby naturally, she was all in. And so was I.

Joey started reading everything she could read about midwives and home births. She wasn't a reader, but she became one then. She watched every documentary she could find and found websites to learn all she could learn. She found out that the most famous midwifery birthing center in the world was called The Farm, and it was only an hour from our house, in Summertown, Tennessee. She read all about it, how it got started in the early 1970s with a bunch of hippies in buses who had moved there from San Francisco to get back to the land. Back to the way it was. And it appealed to Joey, and to me too. Joey learned all about the women who started it, about Ina May and Pamela and a couple of others, and she found a phone number and left a message, hoping to get Pamela as her midwife. And she did.

Miss Pamela was about seventy years old by the time she came into our life. She had delivered hundreds, if not thousands, of babies in the last forty years, the natural way . . . the way God had intended it to be, Joey told me, while reading to me one day. Joey and Pamela became fast friends. They were like kindred spirits, and with Pamela by her side, Joey's fear of having a baby was replaced by excitement. By the anticipation of a beautiful life-changing experience that was coming. Joey looked forward to her monthly visits to The Farm, to have Pamela and the other midwives press on her tummy and listen to the baby's heartbeat.

When the big day came, Joey was making breakfast for her mom and me (June had come to visit and help as the baby's delivery got closer) when, all of a sudden, she excused herself and headed to the bathroom. Within minutes Joey was timing her contractions and writing them down on a sheet of notebook paper. Pamela arrived about an hour or so after the close contractions began, and within the hour Joey had dilated to eight centimeters and was soon ready to have the baby. In checking to see if Joey's water had broken, Pamela realized that that baby had turned and was about to be born breech. She reassured Joey that she could do it, that this was what she was born to do, and everything was going to be all right. And it was.

Indiana was born with no complications. All eight pounds and two ounces of her. Pamela said the baby was healthy and strong, and though Joey had dreaded how hard having a baby would be physically, she absolutely loved the birth experience. Many, many times, to whoever would listen, Joey would say it was the greatest thing she had or would ever do in her life.

Within a week Joey was sitting on the couch beside me with Indy in her arms, saying, "Now I see why people want to have more of these. I would have five more if God would let me." I was shocked. So surprised by how strong she'd been in facing her greatest fears and, even more so, by how much her heart had melted. How clear it was to see that her greatest fear was becoming her greatest joy. It was a God thing for sure, and we both knew it. Something that I could only understand looking through the lens of faith. How God seems to do things.

When you die, to self . . . it's then that you truly live. And for the first time in her life, I could tell Joey was really living. She was complete with that baby in her arms. Something had been missing from her life, and now she knew what it was. A baby. Complete trust in God. For her, they were the same thing, actually. And I was so honored to watch it all unfold right in front of me.

I was also honored to be a father again. Papa, actually. I had asked Joey if it would be okay if we could have me be Indiana's papa, instead of daddy or dad or any other term of endearment. I will always be Heidi and Hopie's daddy, but I am Indy's papa. The same, but different. A lot older for sure with Indiana and, hopefully, a little wiser and smarter about what's important in life and what's not. I was excited to see where this new phase of our lives would lead. Both Joey and I were.

First to have love. To be with Joey. And then to have something so good and beautiful. That was more than I ever imagined. A career, and now a baby. I was in total awe of what God had done with my life and ours over the last dozen years.

I still am.

Forty-Nine

LIFE IS COMPLICATED

This brand-new life, our precious baby girl, had arrived safe and sound and without a hitch. Or so we thought . . .

We kissed and held each other for a long, long time just after the baby was born. It was the longest, sweetest kiss I think Joey and I ever shared. Pamela put the baby in Joey's arms, and the world stood still. Heidi, Hopie, June, the midwives, and I knew that this was a special moment. And we all basked in it.

Within a few minutes they started cleaning up the baby and Joey. I was busy taking pictures and staring at the baby, so I didn't notice the concern on Pamela's face at first. I went out into the kitchen and made a few calls to tell Joey's daddy and sisters and my family that a baby had been born and both she and her mama were doing great. At least, I thought they were . . . but I would soon find out otherwise.

Something in Pamela's eyes showed concern for Indiana's eyes. And there was more. Joey's body wasn't following through the way it should. The placenta wasn't passing, and it had been a good while. Pamela was very concerned. She came and got me and told me that she wanted to call an ambulance to transport Joey to the hospital. I asked if it was serious and if Joey was going to be okay, and she said yes, it could be, but all should be fine if we could act fast.

Twenty minutes later Joey was strapped onto a stretcher that was being wheeled out the front door of our farmhouse. I walked beside her and talked with her and told her everything was going to be okay. She just smiled up at me, sure that it would be too. Pamela rode in the back of the ambulance with Joey and the paramedics, and our older girls and I followed behind them in our SUV. It was such a mad rush to get out of the house, we hadn't found the baby's car seat, so I held Indiana in my arms as Heidi drove. She was barely a half-hour old.

When we got to the hospital, I walked the halls with Indy in my arms, looking for my wife's room. When I finally found it, a nurse told me I needed to wait outside. They were working on her and would let me know soon how it was going. Minutes later I was still outside Joey's room but sitting on the floor now, the baby still in my arms, and sobbing. I could hear Joey screaming in pain at the top of her lungs. I kept thinking, *They're hurting her! Don't they realize that?* I was getting angry. Finally, I couldn't wait any longer, and I handed the baby to the girls and burst through the door into the hospital room. I ran to my wife's side, and someone handed me a mask to put on. I held Joey's hand and stroked her face as she cried and screamed. It was terrible.

The doctor who was on duty was having to do a D&C, and evidently there had been no time for anesthesia. At least that's what I heard, and what it sounded like. Joey was in terrible pain, and she was scared, and so was I. Finally, after what seemed like forever, the ordeal was over. The doctor said the surgery had been a success and Joey was resting, or trying to.

I stayed by her side as nurse after nurse came in, taking Joey's vital signs and making sure she was okay. I could see them glancing over at Indiana in my arms. At some point the doctor came in the room and asked me if I could come outside and speak with her. I thought she was going to talk with me about them possibly doing a blood transfusion because Joey had lost so much in the surgery. But, instead, the doctor said, "Mr. Feek, I think there's a strong possibility that your baby has Down syndrome." I thought I was in the twilight zone.

At first I didn't respond. I just stared at her. *Did I just hear what I think I heard?* Finally I said, "What makes you say that?" The doctor explained that she was concerned about the shape of Indiana's eyes, the extra skin in the back of her neck, and the single line across the palm of her hand, among other things. All those signs pointed to Down syndrome, she said, and she thought we should have her genetically tested in the coming days.

I was still in shock. Everything had turned so quickly, from a perfect pregnancy and by-the-book home birth, to Joey being in emergency surgery and our baby possibly having Down syndrome. It was almost too much for me to take in. Too much to process.

When I got back in the room, I held our baby and looked at her. Really looked at her. Looking for the things the doctor had mentioned. I could see that she was right about some of them, but I still couldn't wrap my mind around the possibility of that really being the case. That our child could have Down syndrome.

Not only had we never done any testing while Joey was pregnant, we had no real doctor appointments or scans at all. We didn't need to. We chose a different path. Complete faith. We didn't want to know if it was a boy or a girl, and we wouldn't have wanted to know if the baby had Downs or anything else. Though we never actually considered that our child would be anything less than perfect, it honestly wouldn't have mattered if we had known. We would have believed that the baby we have is the baby we're supposed to have. But that doesn't change the fact that it came as quite a shock to me, and I knew it would be for Joey too. I had no idea how I was going to tell her.

She slept a long time after the surgery. She so needed the rest. When she woke, I was still by her side. I put the baby in her arms, and she was so glad to see her and hold her again. And while she stroked Indy's soft dark hair, I explained what the doctor had told me. Joey listened and hardly looked up. She just stared at Indiana and took it all in. When I finished talking, all she said was, "She's beautiful, isn't she?" And she was. That was all Joey felt. All that I felt. I think it was important to her, and to me, to stay in the moment. Not to let our fears or concerns run away with us. We just stayed there. In the magic of God giving us the most beautiful little baby girl that we'd ever seen. And that was enough.

A day later Joey got to come home. It had been a difficult twenty-four hours for my wife, and what she needed more than anything was to be home. To once again be in the shelter of the farmhouse we loved and the life we knew. To just be a family. And though there had been complications and we had no idea what they meant or what was in store for us or Indiana, we were excited and thankful. So thankful that God had blessed us with a healthy child and that Joey could have her at home, naturally. That meant so much to her.

Fifty

FAME TO FARM

We had decided to take time off. A whole year: 2014. To let the applause die down and do nothing but be together and raise our baby. And write about it.

We were hoping that by springtime we would have much more than vegetable seeds planted firmly in the ground that was ours. We wanted to dig in too. To be a bigger part of the land and have that little piece of earth be a bigger part of us. We thought we were going to spend the year homesteading. Joey and me and the baby. And I was going to blog about it.

—✕—

I hadn't been writing songs for a while. A year or more. I had been busy. We all had. Making a TV show at home: *The Joey + Rory Show*. From 2012 until the beginning of 2014, we made fifty-two episodes. The show was a way to make and share our music with the world. And to do it *our* way. From our farmhouse to theirs. To millions of living rooms across the country every Friday night. It was an idea that I had come up with, and we had somehow pulled it off—with the help of some friends here in Nashville, who would bring their film skills, and some other friends in Texas, who had the financial resources to make it happen. The show was a huge success and later would go into syndication; it's still playing in reruns, even now. Our hope was that it wouldn't be just a television show about today. It was our own little *Andy Griffith Show* set to music. Something that could be around awhile. Maybe even after we were gone.

But for me, it was more than that. Much more. Going from farm to fame wasn't all it was cracked up to be. And it had taken its toll on my wife by 2011. I wanted to find a way to make my wife's dreams come true while, at the same time, give her the ability to wake up and water her garden and feed her chickens every day. It was my effort to have it all. And we did, with the TV show. Or pretty darn close to it. But even more than that, it was another way for me to capture that time in our lives and keep it forever. All of our music and all of our music videos were directly or indirectly about our lives. Filmed here at home, using what we had as a backdrop for the story we were telling. It was important to me to capture our lives on film. I knew these moments wouldn't last forever, but then again . . . maybe they could. And so, in making our television show, I wanted a part of each episode to be about what was going on in our lives—what parts of the world we had traveled to, or the homemade soap Joey was making with the neighbor lady. I captured it all, including our community. My sister Marcy and the restaurant, our neighbors, and our handyman, Thomas. They are all still here. Forever sealed in time in episodes of our TV show. And so are Joey and I and our girls. Those moments in time have stopped and will last forever.

But for now, the show was over. I had decided to take a break from it. To walk away and welcome something else. Our baby. And a simpler life. Joey wanted it too. She was ready. And the time was upon us.

My wife encouraged me to start writing about our lives in a different way than I had before. With a blog. To continue capturing our lives and the moments I wanted us to remember, but doing it with my pen, mostly, and some pictures. So I figured out how to create a blog, and I titled it "This Life I Live." I launched it online and started telling our story as it was happening, sharing it with whoever happened to stumble upon it. At the same time, I started filming our lives even more than usual. I filmed every day, not for a TV show or a music video. But for us. For some reason—that I wouldn't come to understand for two more years—I felt that writing the blog and filming our lives in detail that year was important.

I had no earthly idea how very important it would be. To me. To Joey. And to the whole world.

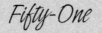

Fifty-One

TURN, TURN, TURN

The baby was here, and spring had sprung. New life was everywhere. And my wife was beyond excited about it. So was I.

In what seemed like the blink of an eye, Joey had gone from not wanting babies to thinking maybe we should have more of them. And that was blowing my mind! We had quite a few conversations about it. She was seriously considering it if God would let it happen. She loved having Indiana that much. And it was clear that being a mama was what she was born to do.

But we wanted to be responsible, so we made an appointment to visit with Dr. Marchman—the doctor who had helped her in the hospital a few weeks ago after the complications from the home birth. Joey liked her and decided to start seeing her. Joey's hope was to get back on birth control, only for a short while, while we continued thinking and praying about the possibility of having another baby. She felt like maybe she should have more, but she wanted to be sure . . . and even more so, to take it to God in prayer.

By the time Joey came out of her appointment, her prayer had been answered.

As Joey walked toward the truck, she looked a little dazed. I had driven down the street to pick up two coffees for us, and the baby was asleep in the backseat as Joey opened her door and sat down. "The doctor says there's a small mass on my cervix," she said. "She is worried that it might be cancer."

I tried to process what she had just said but couldn't really. It was too foreign. Too strange. We had a brand-new, beautiful baby in the car with us, and we were thinking of having more. "I'm sure it's nothing, honey," I told her. And I reached for her hand and put it in mine, the way I had done thousands of times. And Joey smiled, and so did I. Both wanting to believe it. Needing to believe it.

The doctor had done a biopsy, and in a few days she said she would call us to let us know the results. So Joey and I went on with life as normal, not giving it much more thought until the next day when Joey woke up from her nap and had a voice message on her phone. It wasn't from Dr. Marchman; it was from a cancer oncologist wanting to set up an appointment for Joey to come in for a consultation. Joey immediately called her doctor, who said she wanted to talk to us in person.

When we got to Dr. Marchman's office and sat with her, she was mortified to learn that the oncologist had called us before giving her the chance to explain the results. And then she broke down crying. It was surreal. We didn't know her, really, and here we were in her office, trying to help her keep it together. "It's okay," Joey said to her. "Just tell us. It's okay."

"I'm so sorry," the doctor said as she wiped her tears. "It's cancer." And through her tears she proceeded to tell us that the biopsy had come back positive and that Joey had something called squamous cell carcinoma. Cervical cancer. She explained that we would need to see a cancer specialist in Nashville, who would help us decide the best path to take— whether chemo or radiation or surgery or all three.

We left her office that day in a daze. Silently riding home. Not really sure what to feel. Again, I reached for her hand and said what I believed to be true: That everything was going to be okay. That I was sure they had caught it early and it would be something that would probably just be a small bump in the road. Things would be back to normal in no time.

"No more babies," Joey said, as a tear rolled down her cheek. I just smiled and told her that we already had the greatest baby. And that she was enough. And I knew she was. Indiana was a gift that neither of us ever expected to have ... how could we be disappointed not to have more?

God had answered our prayer.

When we got home, we knelt down in front of the couch, with our baby in Joey's arms, and prayed again. This time for God to be with us through whatever was headed our way. To be with Joey as we met with more doctors and learned more about the cancer that was in her body and how to get rid of it. To be with me as I walked with her. And to be with our baby as we raised her. Prayer has a way of comforting a heart. Of making fear subside and hope rise. At least for us it always has.

That was in May 2014, and our garden would have to wait. All the plans we had to homestead and dig deeper roots in our soil were put on hold for a while. Instead, we would spend the summer in meetings with oncologists and radiologists and surgeons. Taking PET scans and CT scans and learning more than we ever wanted to know about cancer.

And Joey would go through another surgery—this time a radical hysterectomy—and spend weeks recovering at home before she would find herself in the garden and spending time with the baby chicks that she loved so much.

By late July, Joey's health was being restored, and so was our hope. And our little Indiana had provided so much joy through it all. She is what Joey lived for. My wife fell more and more in love with being a mama every day. And more in love with her baby. It was easy to see, even within the first couple of months, that Indy had personality and was filled with so much love. And that love overflowed, spilling into every room of our farmhouse and every part of our lives.

That fall and first Christmas with Indy was magical for us. Though we'd had a scary moment, it had made us stronger and helped us put our lives in perspective even more. We savored our time together, those moments we got to spend. And though the surgery and recovery time weren't easy for Joey, she had gotten through it, and it was all behind her.

At least we thought it was.

Fifty-Two

UPS AND DOWNS

I don't know why God gave us a child with Down syndrome.

I guess it could just be random. The luck of the draw. Maybe our chances were greater because Joey was in her late thirties when Indy was born. But I doubt it's that. I know it's not. We have the baby we have because God wanted us to have her. I don't mean that in a "God's got a plan" sort of way. I mean it in a "He knew we needed this child" way. Or, at least, He knew that I did.

I have a feeling—I've had it for a while now—that Indiana is here to teach me something. To teach me everything. She's going to be different from our two older girls. And that difference is, more than likely, exactly what I need, so I can learn what I don't know. So I can grow in the ways that I need to grow. I have no doubt that Indiana is going to show me how to get over myself. How to just *be*. And to be comfortable with who I am. Something that is still hard for me at fifty-one. She's going to teach me what unconditional love is. What it really is. Not the version that I want it to be.

I might be wrong about these things, but I doubt it. More than likely, she will teach me things I don't have any idea yet that I even need to learn. Important things. She will teach all of us. Just because she's different. Her extra chromosome will be the thing that changes our DNA. What we're made of and what's down deep inside.

Fifty-Three

HURT PEOPLE HURT PEOPLE

Hurt people hurt people. I heard that phrase at a church service in Nashville in the latter part of the nineties. I thought it was catchy, but I didn't really understand it at the time. Not until later that year, when I came to realize what that line really meant. And what it means still. Those four words have probably helped me not to hold grudges more than anything else.

—ɯ—

I was spending most of my time writing songs in those days. Telling stories, doing what I loved most to do. On one particular day I was writing with a legendary songwriter named Richard Leigh. He was twenty or so years my senior and had written some of the country music classics of my childhood—"Don't It Make My Brown Eyes Blue" and "The Greatest Man I Never Knew," to name a couple. By then, I was writing for Harlan Howard and had turned the garage building behind their publishing company into my office and writing room. Richard was a kind man. Handsome, with a warm smile and a gentle spirit. I liked him immediately.

We spent most of that morning together not writing a song. Instead, just talking. Mostly him asking questions and me answering them. I think he was trying to get to know me. What I was about. Who I was, really.

"Where did you grow up?" he asked. "How many kids do you have?" And the list of questions went on and on. I told him all about how I'd moved to Nashville with my two girls in '94, then had to move back to Texas, then finally came to Nashville to stay in the fall of 1995. He asked lots of questions about them. About my daughters. "Where's their mother?" he asked. "Do they ever get to see her?" And a hundred others. I could tell where he was going with his questioning, or at least I thought I could. I explained to him that the girls' mother lived in Florida somewhere, and we really didn't ever hear from her.

"That's terrible," he finally said. "It's so, so very sad."

"No," I told him. "It's okay. We have a good life. The girls and I."

"I'm not talking about you," he said. "I'm talking about their mother. How incredibly difficult it must be to wake up every day and carry the burden of leaving them."

I was shocked. Devastated. No one had ever said anything like that to me before. They'd only seen my side of the story, felt bad for me and bad for the girls. But not Richard. He immediately recognized a deeper wound that someone other than me was carrying around. A pain that I have never had to bear for one day, let alone years at a time. And he was right. Their mother has had to carry those choices on her shoulders for years and carries them still. That's a burden that I don't know. Thank God.

Richard and I didn't write a song that day. We actually have never written one together since then either. But I took something away from that time we spent together that was better than even the greatest of songs. Perspective. He gave me the gift of seeing their mother's side of our story. And it's why I am unable to put her at fault. For any of it, really. I feel for her greatly.

She came through Nashville once, a year or so after that day I spent with Richard. She had called a few days before and said she'd be passing through and wanted to see the girls. Her girls. It had been six or seven years since she'd seen or talked to them. I asked Heidi and Hopie if they wanted to see her, and they said yes. So she came and sat in the gazebo at the apartment complex that we lived in at the time and waited with me for the bus to drop the girls off after school. They slowly walked up to her, their Hello Kitty packs on their backs and grade-school books in their hands. She gave them hugs and introduced them to the littler girl who was with her. Their half sister. We hadn't known about her. In time, their mother would have another child, too, my girls would learn.

They spent the afternoon together, talking. And some of the next day. Playing Putt-Putt golf and having lunch with this stranger who was their mom. Hopie hadn't seen her since she was eighteen months old, and Heidi was a little over three. They didn't remember her. And in the end, they said they felt like she was a cousin of mine that they'd heard about but not met. They were glad to see her but didn't feel anything when she left again. That would turn out to be a good thing, I think.

She made them promises. That they would keep in touch. That she'd send birthday cards and Christmas gifts. But those cards and gifts never came.

She would come again to visit them. Ten years later, after friending Heidi on Myspace. The girls were now eighteen and twenty years old, looking at the stranger who had carried them and loved them when they were little and moved on. It was a good visit. Followed by more promises made and even more of them broken.

It hurt them. It hurts them still, I think. But I have tried to encourage them to see what Richard saw all those years ago. Though their pain is great, their mother's pain is probably greater. And they understand that.

Like all of us, she is doing the best she can with what she has.

I know she is.

Fifty-Four

JOSEPHINE

In March 2015, I moved to Virginia for another girl. Her name was Josephine.

And it wasn't just me who moved. So did Joey, Indy, and a bunch of our friends. We didn't really move there, but we might as well have. We were gone from home for three months, and by the time we got back, I had been through so much—creatively—that I felt like I was coming to Tennessee to visit friends, not moving back to the house and life that were mine. Ours. It was so strange.

We were there to make a movie: *Josephine.* As we loaded our Suburban and headed east that day in March, we had no idea what "making a movie" meant exactly, but we were about to find out. It would mean scores of sleepless nights, enduring and working through levels of stress that I didn't even know were possible for the human body. But it was also the single greatest creative endeavor that I've ever been a part of. Everything else I'd done before paled in comparison.

And Joey's role in the film? It was to be the writer and director's wife. To support her husband. And she loved it. That wasn't the role I gave her. That was the job she wanted. She loved being in the background for a change. Knowing that for the first time in a long time, it wasn't really about her or our careers. It was about someone else: Josephine.

The film we were making was the story of a woman who is the wife of a Civil War soldier. She is on a great quest to find the husband she hasn't heard from in more than a year. She cuts off her hair, puts on his clothes, and joins the army disguised as a man, then fights her way across the country in search of the man she loves. We were there in Virginia for her. To tell her story. To be a part of something we'd never been part of before. Making a film.

I think that period of time that wasn't about my wife, or about us, was great for both Joey and me. It was about something bigger. Something that took a community to make. Not only did we move there to make the movie, but so did Heidi and Hopie; our bus driver, Russell; our manager (and the cowriter of the film with me), Aaron; and a half dozen or so other friends from our little community. It was not only amazing to have the chance to make a film, but to make it with people I love was even more special. And at that time in my life to boot. The day before I said, "Action!" for the first time, I turned fifty. It was an incredible gift to have the chance to learn something new at that age. I felt like I was young again . . . like when I first arrived in Nashville with a guitar and a dream. What a blessing to start following a brand-new dream when you're fifty years old.

Joey cooked for the crew and made dinners for the main cast members, who came to the 1830s plantation house where we stayed just before we started shooting. She loved being behind the scenes and doing what she could. Having her come on set with the baby and visit me every day was so grounding. It helped me to keep in mind what was most important, even when my mind was overwhelmed with the task in front of me each day.

We wrapped shooting in mid-May and brought a couple of hard drives full of footage back to our home in Tennessee. I was going to spend the summer editing the movie in the film-editing suite we had built in the milk house on our property. Our hope was that the film would turn into something special and lead somewhere wonderful. That's still our hope.

It felt so good to be back home. Joey and Indy had made a couple of trips back to Tennessee in April and early May to get some seeds started in the garden, and we were excited to start digging in the dirt and really spending the summertime enjoying the baby and our lives together at the farm. We had no idea that this would be our last summer together.

Fifty-Five

SOMETHING WORSE

S he was sick and tired of being sick and tired.

     While in Virginia, and even before that, Joey had been feeling bad. Not terrible, just nauseous at times. She was having some trouble with her bowels, and no matter what she did, it just didn't seem to go away. She wasn't worried about it, though; or if she was, she never let it show. She just kept trying new things to help with what she thought was an intestinal bug or virus. Diet, essential oils, supplements . . . natural things. Joey was always for finding a natural way to heal the body before going to see doctors or taking medicine. It's just who she was, and I love her for it. She knew what a big business the pharmaceutical world is and that there are many things we can do ourselves to turn our health problems around without prescription drugs, and she loved the challenge and discipline of trying to figure it out.

But what was happening to her wasn't getting any better. She went to see a doctor in April, and he tested all of her blood levels and said they were normal. So she kept cooking and cleaning and being a mama and living a regular life. I was worried about her and told her so. But she'd just smile that smile that said everything's gonna be fine, and I wanted to believe her, but something inside me wasn't so sure.

A few weeks after we came home from Virginia, I took Joey to see a GI doctor at Vanderbilt. He did a colonoscopy, and the baby and I sat in the recovery room with Joey awaiting the results. Joey was playing with

Indiana on her lap when the doctor came in. The look on his face was one of concern. We really weren't prepared for what he told us, that there seemed to be a mass on part of her colon, and he recommended she get full scans done and go back and see her oncologist. When we got home that night, as Joey and Indy slept, I googled some of the words the doctor had said that afternoon. *Sigmoid colon.* Four-centimeter mass. I held my breath and typed *cervical cancer return statistics* and hit enter. I didn't like what it said, so I closed my laptop and started praying.

I didn't tell Joey that the numbers weren't good. I couldn't. Besides, we weren't sure that it actually was cancer. Within a day or two, though, we would be. I still remember Joey and me being on the phone with her oncologist, Dr. Wheelock, as he explained what he saw on the scans. And as he told us about the chemo and radiation regimen that he recommended, we listened, but neither of us really believed it. I'm not one to beat around the bush, so I just asked him, "John, should we be worried?" He said, "Yes. You should be very worried."

Just as summer was about to begin, it was over. We knew it was. There would be no gardening or baby chicks or editing the movie or anything else for a while. This was going to be our life. Fighting for her life was going to be our life.

Ultimately, we decided on Cancer Treatment Centers of America, in Zion, Illinois, outside Chicago, to get treatment for the cancer that had returned. We loved their holistic approach, that they incorporated so much more in their treatments. Most of all, faith. They believed in the power of God and embraced it. We needed that. We needed doctors and staff around us who would not only provide the finest health care for Joey but also pray for her.

Another reason we chose CTCA is they wanted to do surgery. To try to remove it. All the other places didn't. They just wanted to do chemo and radiation and see what would happen. We understood enough about Joey's condition to know that if the mass wasn't removed, we had little chance of stopping it from growing.

The morning of the surgery—to remove the mass and a few organs that we would learn were filled with cancer—Joey and I lay in a hotel bed with Indy beside us. We held hands, and we prayed. We prayed with all we had. That God would let this surgery go well and that the doctors could get it all . . . and that Indiana could get to grow up with a mama. That was the part that was the hardest for us to swallow. It would be for anyone. How could God give her this precious gift, then take it all away? There weren't enough tissues to handle our tears that morning. But still, we both had faith. We believed He could heal Joey, with or without the surgery. We knew it. And we also knew that we were not here in this place, going through this, by accident.

She looked at me and said, "This is the day the Lord has made."

And it was.

It was a hard, hard day that He had made. With many harder ones to follow.

Fifty-Six

SURGERY AND MORE

The surgery took almost ten hours.

I waited and I paced and I prayed and I drank black coffee 'til I was sick with worry. Finally the doctor came out and sat beside me on a padded chair in the waiting room. "It went well," he said. "I think we got most of it." He told me how they'd found more cancer than they thought, and they had to remove her bladder, among other things. She was in recovery and would be for the next few hours. He was still talking when I jumped ahead.

"Will she be okay?" I asked.

"I hope so," the doctor answered.

That wasn't the answer I wanted. So then I asked, "Do you think it will come back?"

"Yes," he answered. "I'm sorry."

What? What was he talking about? Why had she just gone through all of this . . . ten hours of surgery . . . and God knows how much pain . . . if it was going to come back?

He explained that this was a radical approach—that they and we had chosen this plan for trying to get out all the cancer and stopping it in its tracks—and it either would work or it wouldn't. And if it didn't work, at least her body had been "reset" to where it had been before the cancer came back, and her quality of life would be better.

I still didn't understand. You don't talk about "quality of life" to someone whose wife is going to live. *How can this be?* I thought. *It's just a setback. She has to get better.*

In the prep room before her surgery, Joey had sung to me. To Indiana and me. The old hymn "I Need Thee Every Hour." The same song she had sung a year before, facing the same fears in a different city with a different surgical team. And again this time, as her tears fell and made the words hard to understand, the song comforted her. And me. Hymns always did. It's why she and I later that summer made an album filled with nothing but hymns. Tracking the musicians in Nashville and recording her vocals in hotel rooms whenever she was up for singing. And then filming a TV special in September, when the chemo and radiation had zapped the cancer and all of her energy and she could barely stand. She wanted to make that record. It was important to her. To sing those songs and have them recorded for Indiana and for our older girls and for the whole world to hear. They had helped her and were helping her now. Maybe they could help others.

—⁂—

What that doctor had said in the waiting room after Joey's surgery rocked me. For the next few days I walked around like a zombie, trying to process what was happening. The truth of it. Joey and I had never considered that she might not make it through all this, not really. And I wasn't ready to start thinking that way now. Neither was she.

It would be nearly ten days before we would go home, and Joey would start the recovery process at the farmhouse. By the time she started making a comeback, she was barely over a hundred pounds. The surgery and the stress of it all had taken its toll. She slept and slept, and when she was awake, she didn't have the energy to get out of bed or do much of anything. Weeds took over the garden. Joey's mama and neighbors filed in by the dozens to help. To do what they could. Make dinners, weed, and pick the tomatoes. Anything we needed.

Finally Joey began improving, and her smile and spirit started to return. Just in time for the next phase. Six weeks of chemo and radiation. This time we chose to go to the Cancer Treatment Center in Atlanta. Actually, an hour south of Atlanta, in the small town of Newnan. It was closer, only four hours away, and we could probably come home on a weekend or two. That would be something for her to look forward to. Me too.

At first we stayed in a hotel. For two weeks we lived out of suitcases, and Indy spent her afternoons in the pool with her papa while her mama slept or sat on a chair in the shade, watching her baby, but not having the energy to do much with her. Joey had radiation every day and chemo once a week for this round, and it was again taking its toll on her. She was spent.

I tried to keep life as normal as possible for her and lay beside her in the evenings after Indy went to sleep, and we would talk about our lives before all this happened. About all our adventures on the road playing music and about the things she wanted to do in the future. The cows she wanted to raise for beef and the strawberries she wanted to pick with Indiana. Reliving the past and dreaming about the future somehow seemed to help. It helped us forget that we weren't living the life we wanted and that it might be this way for a while.

After a few weeks the hospital moved us into a house. A beautiful split-level home only a couple of miles from the treatment center. That made things easier. It felt like a home, even if it wasn't ours. Indy was growing and learning sign language by that time, and her little personality was starting to show itself. She would find a way to make her mama smile, even on the hardest of days. Again and again, Indiana would provide joy and perspective that we had a hard time finding on our own. She was so sweet and so fun, and the daily work of caring for her needs took my mind off the things that I had no answers for . . . like what tomorrow held. Routine things like changing diapers and getting Indy down for her nap time always helped get our minds off the harder things—the pain and suffering Joey was going through.

We made a few trips home during that time. Twice, I think. One was to play a weekend of sold-out shows at our farmhouse concert hall. I always told Joey we could cancel them at any time, but she looked forward to those ninety minutes. To being on the stage and letting the music and lyrics take her far away from where she'd been all summer and where we'd be heading back on Sunday afternoon.

The other trip back home was for her fortieth birthday. I had gotten Joey a horse. Two of them, actually. Since having a horse of her own named Velvet when she was a little girl, Joey had always wanted another one—but the timing was never right. Joey had always said we weren't home enough and we didn't have a good place to keep one or a million other good reasons not to make it happen. I couldn't wait any longer. Now was gonna have to be the time. *Now or never*, I thought. Some wonderful friends in Texas gave me the horses for Joey, and they sent them in a trailer with their trainer, Chico. We had a party for Joey in the front yard. It was a beautiful day, and quite a few of Joey's friends and family were there. She loved the blue and red roans when our friend Cowboy Jack led them out into the front yard. "They're perfect, honey," Joey said. "They're just perfect." She even got up on one of them, Blue Moon, and we took a few pictures. But something inside her knew it would be a long, long time, if ever, before she would be able to ride again.

The horses were a dream come true for her. But Joey had bigger dreams to deal with now. And they had to do with living. Just being able to wake up and see her baby smile and hold her husband's hand. That was what she was dreaming of now. And through the twenty-five rounds of radiation and the weeks of chemo, she never lost hope. She kept believing that she would get better.

Unfortunately, that wasn't a dream that I could make come true for her, no matter how much I tried.

It was in God's hands. Not mine.

Fifty-Seven

NO MORE

In mid-October, we had only been back home for a week or so, when the doctors in Atlanta wanted Joey to come back down so they could do some scans to see how her body was responding to the surgery and the first six weeks of chemo and radiation. It was pretty much a formality; they already had the next round of chemo set up. This next one would be stronger and tougher on her. She would lose her hair and be even sicker. It was hard for me to imagine Joey getting much sicker than she'd been or even surviving another round. The first one, along with the surgery, had been so very hard on her.

We decided that I would stay home and Joey would fly down with her mama. A quick overnight trip, and then they'd be back. They would do the testing that afternoon, then get the results the next morning, and do the next round of chemo in the afternoon before catching a flight home. I kept Indy at the farmhouse with me, and late that evening Joey and I talked on the phone after her scans were done. We were both hopeful and felt almost certain that she would receive good news the next morning and be back home by dinnertime. But it didn't work out that way.

My cell phone rang while I was feeding Indy her breakfast. "It's not good, honey," Joey said.

"What's not good?" I asked. And then there was silence. I could hear her on the other end, trying to fight back the tears, struggling to talk to me. "It's gonna be okay, Joey," I reassured her. "Just tell me what's going on."

229

Joey sturdied herself and continued. "The cancer has continued to grow. They said that even after the surgery and the chemo and radiation . . . it's still spreading."

Again, time seemed to stand still. I could suddenly hear the sound of the clock ticking on the wall near the kitchen. How could this be? This stuff only happened to other people. But I knew the truth of it. *We* are the other people, to other people. Joey told me that the doctors still wanted to keep the same plan and start the new chemo that day to see if they could stop it with stronger drugs.

It took all I had to hang up the phone. To leave her by herself. But I knew it would only be for a little while. "I'm getting in my truck now. I'll be there shortly . . . I love you." And I heard her sweet voice say the same to me: "I love you too."

Within five minutes, Indy was in her car seat, and we were on the road. A million thoughts raced through my mind on the way down to CTCA in Georgia. We had believed that Joey was going to be better. We just knew it. We weren't prepared for anything else. I kept trying to figure out why all the treatment hadn't worked. *Did we choose the wrong place or the wrong path to go down?*

There were so many questions running around in my head, but there was one in particular that I couldn't stop wondering about. *Was this new chemo actually going to help? Had Joey asked the doctor that question?*

When I got to the hospital, I almost ran, with Indy in the stroller, to the chemotherapy wing where Joey was getting the new drugs intravenously. She broke down in tears when she saw me, and her mama took Indy for a walk so we could be alone.

I held her as she sat in the chair and cried. And then I asked her the question I had been thinking about. No, she said she hadn't thought to ask the doctor that. A minute later I was dialing her doctor's cell number from Joey's phone. I walked out in the hallway and asked, "Do you think this is going to help my wife, honestly?" I think the doctor was surprised by my candor.

"No, I don't," she replied.

"Well, why in the world would you have her take it then—after all she's been through?" I asked.

"It might add a little bit more time," she said.

"Add more time? More time to what?" I continued.

"To the six to nine months she has right now," she said.

And there it was. The truth.

In all the time we had been going through this, no one had ever told us that Joey was terminal. Not once. They said that it could be, that it might turn into terminal cancer . . . but never that it *was*. As my mind raced back over the last few months, I found myself replaying many of the conversations we'd had with all of Joey's doctors. Had they all been saying the same thing this whole time? Saying it, without saying it? Just being nice to us? If they all knew that and had been telling us that, we totally missed it. Or our sense of hope overrode it all.

I thanked the doctor for her honesty, then hung up and walked back into Joey's cubicle. I had tears in my eyes now, and she knew what that meant. I told her what the doctor had said, and we both agreed that the best thing to do was turn off the machine and just go home. As we were still talking, trying to sort out what would come next, the machine that had been administering the new chemo into her bloodstream started beeping, indicating that the bag was completely empty.

"Well, there goes my hair," Joey said.

"That's okay," I told her. "You're going to look beautiful bald."

Fifty-Eight

CRYING AND DRIVING

I had been cutting the hay in the back field for the last two hours. It felt good to be on the tractor. Farming. Gentleman farming, my friend called it.

I had been wanting to do this for a long time. Cut hay. And now that we were home, it felt good to be on the tractor, going 'round and 'round on the sixty acres that we had purchased earlier in the year.

Our friend Danny Smith and his nephew had been cutting it and baling it for us all summer, and we were down to just the field directly behind our farmhouse. We needed it cut for the horses. Not for them to eat but to manage how much it had grown and get the big stuff down.

As I circled the field, I watched the house for Joey. She knew what this meant to me. She always knew important things like that, and any other time she would have come outside and watched me, made sure I knew that she was seeing me, and waved. I would have waved back, and this moment would be complete. I have always believed that great moments aren't really great moments unless they're shared. It's as though they need to be acknowledged to be real or something. But she didn't come out and wave, or even come to the window. I just kept going 'round and 'round, and each time the tractor faced the farmhouse, I would look for her.

She was in bed. I knew that. Her sister Julie and her children had come to visit, along with some more of Joey's family. They all had heard the news—that there was no more the doctors could do. Not really. The

233

hospital would be glad to keep pumping her full of poison with hopes that it would turn it around, but it wasn't going to make a difference. We were beat. And they, and now we, knew it.

Then, finally, I saw her. My eyes aren't so good anymore, but I could see that it was her. And she had Indiana in her arms. They came out onto the back porch, then walked down and across the yard toward the horse corral. I smiled big and waved with all I had. *She sees me! She came out!* I thought. And I waved more. But she didn't wave back. I squinted as the tractor chugged closer.

Autumn. It was Joey's thirteen-year-old niece Autumn, not Joey. Autumn had Indy and was looking at the horses. I pulled my arm down and pulled my cowboy hat down over my eyes a bit more and let the breeze come across my face. And as I turned the corner and headed away from the house, I cried. Not like I had before. This time was different. It was a loud, ugly cry. The kind you don't let out with anyone around. The RPMs of the engine drowned out my sorrow so no one could hear, and I let the blades cut the grass and the truth cut through to my heart.

My wife is dying. She's not going to be here to wave to me. I will be alone. Again. With a baby. Again.

A few minutes later I felt a vibration in my overalls pocket. I knew what it was, so I rounded the corner near the horse paddock with the tractor and pulled the clutch and the lever that disengages the PTO and stops the haybine. I slid the reminder away on my phone, climbed down from the New Holland, and trod through the freshly cut grass toward the house.

Five minutes later I whispered to Joey, "She's going to be calling in a minute. Can you wake up and be on this call with me?" She said she could, so I helped her sit up. I sat the phone down between us on the bed while I sat in the rocking chair and pulled my laptop open as the call came in. We put it on speakerphone, and Dr. Kelly Manahan proceeded to give us more details of the scan from the past week.

About more tumors, all around the abdomen area. About two-inch margins and why another surgery wasn't an option. And she told us that cervical cancer is very painful. In the end it is. I had mentioned to her that my mother's pain wasn't too bad when she passed away last year. The doctor explained that this type of cancer is different from what my mother had and why it would be more painful. We needed to stay on top of the pain, she said. That Joey would mostly be sleeping. That medicine was the best way to keep the pain away.

We asked about reprieves and if Joey would get to feel good for a few weeks or months. She said "maybe" with her voice, but I could hear "probably not" in the breath between her words. Joey heard it too. She always had a strong sense of truth and ability to read between the lines. I took notes as the doctor talked. I wanted to make sure I understood how to care for my wife. And how to make sure she had everything she needed. I asked about hospice and getting a hospital bed at the house right away so she could sit up and change positions more easily.

The doctor didn't give us any good news. But she did give us good information, and that was what we needed at the time. When the call was over, Joey said, "I feel relieved in a way. To know there is no hope." She and I talked about everything the doctor had said, and I promised her I would make sure she wouldn't have to feel a lot of pain.

I won't let my wife be hurt anymore. She's been through too much already.

As she laid back down, I knelt beside her, tucking her in. She talked about her anniversary and engagement rings . . . that she wanted our older daughters to have them. And she talked about her life insurance policy and how maybe she could give each of the girls a big chunk to help them get started with their lives. I said that might be nice. Then tears filled her eyes, and she started trying to talk about me moving on when she was gone and finding someone else. I stopped her and said, "No, I don't want to talk about that."

She said, "It's okay, honey. You're still young. You can find someone else and fall in love again."

My tears were falling again now, and though I knew she needed to say those things, I didn't want to hear them.

Not now. Not ever.

Fifty-Nine

INDIANA HOME

I don't do Facebook. I don't really know how. I can get on it and see things, but I don't really know how to navigate it or what the pages are or what they do. Honestly, I don't really want to.

But I knew enough about Facebook that morning in January 2016 to know that we were all over it again. People had reposted the blogs I had written. Joey's story and mine. Individuals, news organizations, *US Magazine*, *People.com*, and many others. Folks took images of Joey and put captions on them that said "Pray for Joey" or something else beautiful. Creations to share.

I sat at the Gaithers' coffee shop in Joey's hometown of Alexandria, Indiana, and thought deeply about what was happening with the story we were sharing and where we were. How kind people the world over had been to us and how something so terrible had turned into something . . . well, beautiful.

Joey had decided to come home to Indiana once we realized that the doctors and hospitals had done all they could. It was only going to be for a few days. Enough time to tell her sisters and mama how much she loved them. To see the old farmhouse that she had grown up in one more time and to say good-bye to the people and town and state that bore her. But a few days turned into a few weeks, then longer. We had been there for three months, and Joey was still doing pretty well, overall. Thinner and weaker, but good . . . depending on the day.

We were now living in a house by a pond, across from Bill and Gloria Gaither. A place where Gloria's mother and father had lived and died. And now it was our turn. Joey's turn. There was a large picture window at the foot of Joey's bed, where she could watch the black and the white swans swim across the icy water and the young deer that she named Daisy stand by the bird feeder, eating corn left for her daily by Bill and his staff. It was a heavenly way to die, if you must. And Joey and I were thankful for it. There wasn't a day that we didn't pinch ourselves for all God had done for us. How precious the time with Joey's family had been. How thankful we all were for the chance to still be together for Christmas and New Year's. The doctors in Indiana were sure that Joey wouldn't make it to Thanksgiving. But she had proved them all wrong and seemed to have found a way to pull the battery out of Old Father Time's clock.

She decided not to return to Tennessee, partly because she was loving being with her family there in Indiana. But also, I think, because she wanted to do this here. Away from our home and our life. To die separate from where we lived. I would rather have been at home, but I didn't mind. I wanted what she wanted. That's all I ever wanted. Down deep. To see my wife happy, like this, at a time when time was running through our fingers like sand. I couldn't have asked for more. Neither could Joey.

Winter was upon us, and though it was terrible, it wasn't so bad. We were together. We had today, and that was enough.

Sixty

SAYING GOOD-BYE

I didn't want to do it. Not ever. I still don't.

But there are times when you have to. You have no choice. Like when Mom loaded us up in her old clunker and moved us from Kansas to Michigan. I didn't want things to change, but they had to. Nothing I could do was going to stop it, so I had to learn to accept it. And so it was with this. Joey and I had been blessed with not only more time together than we thought we might get but also with better time than we ever dreamed was possible. And now that time was about to come to an end.

Joey had called it, back in early November. "I think I'll be here to see Indiana's birthday in February," she said to the roomful of teary-eyed friends who had come up on a bus with our driver, Russell, to tell her good-bye. She was on a high dose of morphine and was slurring her words. After she excused herself and went back into her room to lie down, I felt I should apologize. They could see for themselves now that Joey was nearing the end, and it was heartbreaking to experience. Probably even more heart-wrenching to hear her say that she thought she'd be here another three months. I didn't believe her. None of us did, really. It was the medicine talking, I thought. But it wasn't.

It was Joey talking. That's the kind of resolve my wife has. Like I said, when Joey says something, she means it. She never makes a promise that she doesn't follow through on. And I think this was just another one of those promises. But to me, it was a miracle.

It was now late February, and Joey was still here to sing "Happy Birthday" to our little girl as we all watched her blow out her little "2" candle and rub a paleo cupcake all over her face, laughing and grinning ear to ear. And Joey was here to read our names on the list of nominations that had recently come out for the Grammy Awards. And she was also here to hear the news that our *Hymns* album had been released to much acclaim, and sales numbers had made it the number-one album in America on all charts. She was even here to share a platter full of sushi with me on Valentine's Day as we kissed and said sweet nothings to each other. I got to lie down beside her for a little while and put my arms around her—something that we had not had the opportunity to do in months and months. All we could have hoped for and more had happened in the few months since finding out that the cancer had returned and deciding to embrace the end and not run, not hide from it.

Everything, except for the healing. Except for the miracle. Joey had never stopped believing that it was possible, and she believed it still, right up until then. Her hope was unflappable. When the tumors had grown so large inside her that they were bursting and a terrible discharge was pouring out of her body, she claimed that maybe, just maybe, God was popping them, getting the cancer out. It didn't matter what it was, Joey saw the best in it. The hope in it.

But now, finally, that hope was gone. The day before, we had been rejoicing in all that God had done during this time. How He had been using her story to encourage others and how the new album, filled with the hymns she had grown up with and loved, was doing so well and how the only reason for it was Him. God was going to get all the glory because He was the only way to explain all that was happening. "Isn't it amazing?" I asked her that evening, holding her hand in mine.

She looked at me and said, "Yes . . . so amazing." And then she asked, "Do you think He's going to heal me?"

I didn't want to answer that. But I had to. I couldn't lie to her, not after all she'd been through. "No, honey . . . I don't think He is."

"I didn't think so." And she smiled the softest, kindest smile. "That's okay," she said. "I got to experience everything I wanted to. I was here for our baby's birthday. I'm ready now." And then my wife stopped living.

She didn't die that day, but she quit living. She was still breathing air, and, physically, nothing had changed. Not really. But in another way, everything had. She was ready to go home. To be with her brother, Justin. And to hurt no more. She was tired of hurting.

It was late evening, and Joey's sister Jody, who had become her full-time nurse, was at her son Cody's ball game with the rest of the family. It was just Joey and me. She took my hand and looked me in the eye. "I need you to help me," she said. "Promise me that you will? Promise me, honey . . . I can't do this anymore."

And so I promised her I would. She told me that she had made a decision. No more food, she said. And I knew what that decision meant. No more living. It wasn't much of a sacrifice for her, really, because every time she took even the smallest bite of anything during those last few weeks, and months, actually, she paid a terrible price for it. Her body rejected it, and the pain she had to endure was unbearable. There was no joy in eating, and it was literally the only thing left that she could do.

Once that was gone, there was nothing left. But the future.

It wasn't fast, and it wasn't easy. As a matter of fact, at times, it was beyond terrible. If it had been legal to give my wife a shot, like the vet gave her dog, Rufus, in his last hours, or to push a button that would make her hurting stop, I would've done it. I wouldn't have even blinked. She had already been through too much, and she didn't deserve to go through the pain and agony that the last few days brought. But she did.

Joey was incredibly brave in the end. Brave in how she lived and, even more so, in how she died. It was my honor to be by her side through it all. And to try to put what she, and we, were experiencing into words on my blog and share it with others. She was brave that way too. She didn't have to share what she went through, but she wanted to.

I wrote about the last few months in detail on my blog. It's too much to share here in just one book.

Sixty-One

SECOND GUESSES

After everything that happened and all that Joey went through, people have often asked me, "If you could do it again, would you do anything different?" Well, yes, I would. And I know Joey would too. She told me so. Many times.

We aren't people who second-guess our decisions. We don't think in terms of what-might-have-beens or what-ifs. That's just not how we think. We believe that the choices we've made are the choices we were supposed to make, and they become part of our story . . . how we get to where we are in life. So Joey and I don't have any regrets. That being said, it doesn't mean we wouldn't do things differently if given the chance. The truth is, we would change one thing if we could . . . and one thing we would do exactly the same.

When it comes to living or trying to find a cure to keep living, we would have chosen a different path. But when it comes to dying, we wouldn't have changed anything. The path we took at the end was the right one for us. For Joey.

But the path that got us to that final path, we wouldn't walk down again. At least, I don't think we would.

If God gave us a do-over and we could go back a year in time and be at the place where Joey faced the fact that she might die from cancer, we wouldn't have done the surgery, and Joey wouldn't have done the chemo or radiation. If she could have, I know my wife would've chosen

an even more holistic path than the one we took. One that would've con-
centrated completely on natural ways to try to kill the cancer or stop it
from spreading. And we would've removed the medical path of cutting
and burning and poisoning the body to heal it. In the end, Joey felt like
that practice wasn't the best one. At least not for her. She would've done
little or no medicine and pursued avenues to remove the cancer from her
body naturally.

She would want me to say that. To tell people that. It's not that the
doctors or hospitals that took care of her did anything wrong, because
they didn't. They were all amazing. But she had months and months in
bed to study and read and research possible alternatives, and, in the end,
she thinks some of those alternative approaches are the future. So do I.
For whatever it's worth.

In some ways I think I let my wife down when it came to that. I wish
I was smarter and could've waded through all the options a little better
and helped her make a different decision. But I didn't. I did the best I
could with what I had. And so did my wife.

That truth is still holding true today.

Sixty-Two

LIFE IMITATING ART IMITATING LIFE

Joey took her last breath on this earth on a Friday. The following Tuesday, we laid her down in the soft soil just a few hundred yards from her garden.

She wanted to be there. To be here. And I'm so thankful. From where I sit in our bedroom upstairs at our farmhouse writing this book, I can see her. Or, at least, I can see where she rests. It's the same place where we shot a video a few years ago. It was for a song that we loved and recorded called "When I'm Gone" that a good friend of Joey's wrote. In the video that we made in 2013, we'd painted a picture of a world where I am living here alone, and Joey is buried in that very grove of sassafras trees in the back field. Life imitating art, I think they call it.

It's hard for me to watch it now. That video. But I do. Quite often, actually. And I can't help but see the irony in it. The magic of it. That we recorded a song and made a make-believe video that came true in real life. Nothing is by chance, in my opinion. God knew. And He wanted us to know that He knew. And I think He wanted others to know and see that He is here. Always here with us. All of us.

In the end, I think He wanted me to have Joey singing to me. Sharing the words that He knew I would need to hear from her, for years and years to come.

A BRIGHT SUNRISE WILL CONTRADICT THE HEAVY FOG
    THAT WEIGHS YOU DOWN.
IN SPITE OF ALL THE FUNERAL SONGS, THE BIRDS WILL
    MAKE THEIR JOYFUL SOUNDS.
YOU'LL WONDER WHY THE EARTH STILL MOVES,
YOU'LL WONDER HOW YOU'LL CARRY ON,
BUT YOU'LL BE OKAY ON THAT FIRST DAY WHEN I'M GONE.

DUSK WILL COME WITH FIREFLIES AND WHIP-POOR-WILL
    AND CRICKET'S CALL.
AND EVERY STAR WILL TAKE ITS PLACE IN SILV'RY GOWN
    AND PURPLE SHAWL.
YOU'LL LIE DOWN IN OUR BIG BED, DREAD THE DARK, AND
    DREAD THE DAWN,
BUT YOU'LL BE ALL RIGHT ON THAT FIRST NIGHT WHEN
    I'M GONE.

YOU WILL REACH FOR ME IN VAIN, YOU'LL BE WHISPERING
    MY NAME
AS IF SORROW WERE YOUR FRIEND, AND THIS WORLD SO
    ALIEN.

BUT LIFE WILL CALL WITH DAFFODILS AND MORNING
    GLORIOUS BLUE SKIES.
YOU'LL THINK OF ME, SOME MEMORY, AND SOFTLY SMILE
    TO YOUR SURPRISE.
AND EVEN THOUGH YOU LOVE ME STILL, YOU WILL KNOW
    WHERE YOU BELONG.
JUST GIVE IT TIME, WE'LL BOTH BE FINE WHEN I'M GONE.

AFTER HAPPILY EVER AFTER

There are chapters in a person's life that you don't want to write. Things that you don't want to talk about. I would've thought for me it would be parts of my past that I am embarrassed about or ashamed of. But, strangely, I don't have any problem writing about those things. I can see now where they have led and what they've taught me and how important they are to the bigger story that God has been telling with my life. And my hope is that in my being honest about who I was . . . who I am . . . it might encourage someone, the way that my wife's courage in life and in death has encouraged me and others.

The past is easy for me to write about, but the future is different. It's the unknown. The abyss. A place I've yet to be and a loneliness I've yet to fully experience. I'm not sure I know how to write about that. Or, at least, write about it honestly. But I will try.

We are here. Our little Indiana is in a sweet school about twenty minutes from our farmhouse and is loving it, and I am loving watching her grow and learn new things every day. She is joy. Complete and total love. Even when she's grumpy and throws her sweet potato across the room, all I can do is smile. I believe that Indy is what God has given me to balance the pain. To keep this awful, wonderful life in perspective in a time when the wisdom of His choices are difficult to understand. Indiana's smile erases the questions. It has a way of taking the past and leaving it there and snapping me into the present. Being here, with her, with our older girls . . . right now.

And the work that comes with taking care of a two-year-old by yourself has a way of keeping you from worrying about the future. What life is going to be like for her. For us. They will come—those answers—in time. But for now, I have a baby in a high chair to feed. Baths to run, books to read, and hugs to give. That is all enough.

Joey's garden is in full bloom. It looks beautiful, filled with all the life-giving plants that she loved. I spend most early mornings holding a water hose that is pointed at a row of tomato plants or cabbage or carrots, just as Joey used to do. It's funny, I didn't like it then, when she was here. That was her passion, not mine. I'm ashamed to admit that it was work for me to join her in the garden. To help her weed and harvest and can. Probably much like how it was work for her to sit with me as I was editing music videos or working on something creative. But that's changed now. I like being in the garden. I can see why she loved it.

I do lots of things now that I didn't do before, besides caring for the baby. I am learning to cook again and do piles of dishes and laundry and clean out closets and do things that she gladly made happen all those years without me even knowing how much work it was. And, surprisingly, I've enjoyed it. Most of it, anyway. I can feel the sense of accomplishment that Joey felt in those little things. In taking care of the ones you love. In serving them. The only part that is really hard for me is knowing that I could've done more when she was here. Served her more. Lightened her load. Loved her more. We all want that when someone leaves us, I guess. I know I do.

Sometimes people, complete strangers, will stop me on the street and ask me how I'm doing. I will smile and tell them that I'm doing pretty well, and strangely . . . they won't believe me. They touch my shoulder and lean in. "Are you really?" they say. I find that funny. That people who don't know me know me well enough to ask that. To care. It's beautiful how the Internet—which I mostly dislike—has a way of connecting lives and stories. Of creating relationship, or something very similar.

EPILOGUE

I am grieving. My heart and my soul are in mourning. Still feeling the immeasurable loss of the greatest person that I have ever known, the greatest joy I've ever felt, and the greatest pain I will ever experience . . . all wrapped into one terrible, beautiful thing.

I miss my wife. I am lost without her. Empty again. I haven't been empty like this in a good while. You wouldn't know it to look at me, because my faith is strong and resilient, and I have learned to do what I must do, even when I don't want to. Like moving on with my life. I must. There is no other option. No real one. The baby needs me; my older children need me . . . and I need all of them.

But in the hurt that I feel, there is even greater love. Something that Joey put there. Her, and God. And though she is no longer here with me, her love is. I can feel it. It's tangible and real. It's just as strong as it ever was. Stronger. And it carries me . . . up, up, up. To a place of hope. A hope that this isn't the end of the story. Not by a long way.

Even now, I believe that God is going to give us a great story. Me and Indiana. And our older girls. And when I'm gone, it will be their stories that God is writing. That their lives are telling. And I will have been part of it, just as Joey is part of mine. The best part of mine.

ABOUT THE AUTHOR

RORY FEEK is a true renaissance man, known as one of Nashville's premiere songwriters, entrepreneurs, and out-of-the-box thinkers. He is a world-class storyteller, crossing all creative mediums, from music and film to books and the Internet.

As a blogger, Rory shares his heart and story with the world through thislifeilive.com, which has more than two million Facebook followers. The love story of he and his wife, the story of her battle and loss to cancer, and his vignettes of unwavering faith and hope in the face of tragedy inspire millions of readers.

As a songwriter, Rory has written multiple number-one songs, including Blake Shelton's "Some Beach," Easton Corbin's "A Little More Country Than That," and Clay Walker's "The Chain of Love," and has had dozens of his other songs recorded by Kenny Chesney, Randy Travis, Reba, Trisha Yearwood, Waylon Jennings, and many others.

As an artist, Rory is half of the Grammy-nominated county music duo Joey + Rory. He and his wife, Joey Martin, toured the world, sold hundreds of thousands of records, and have a weekly hit television show that airs all across the country on RFD-TV. Their latest album, *Hymns That Are Important to Us*, sold seventy thousand copies the first week and debuted at number one on Billboard album charts.

As a filmmaker, Rory has directed his first feature-length film, *Josephine*, an epic love story set during the declining months of the

Civil War, with a screenplay he co-wrote with Aaron Carnahan. Rory has three other screenplays in process. He also writes, shoots, and edits Joey + Rory music videos and is the creator of the television shows and specials in which the duo has appeared.

Rory and his two-year-old daughter, Indiana, live an hour south of Nashville in an 1870s farmhouse near their family-owned diner, Marcy Jo's Mealhouse.